Beginner Piano Lessons for Kids

Learn How to Read Sheet Music With Easy
Instructions, Fundamental Exercises to Gain
Confidence and Master The Piano
(Little Maestro Series)

Taylor Kent W.

TABLE OF CONTENTS

INTRODUCTION

Beginner Piano Lessons for Kids

Taylor Kent W.

The piano keys are black and white but they sound like a million colors in your mind.
—Maria Cristina Mena

At the age of eight, I discovered my passion for music when I first picked up the guitar. I was determined to become a rockstar and poured my heart and soul into mastering the instrument, teaching myself how to play. As time passed, I expanded my musical horizons and fell in love with the piano, taking lessons and immersing myself in its beautiful melodies.

As an adult, I've realized that a love for music is one of the greatest gifts we can give to the next generation. That's why I poured my heart and soul into creating *Little Maestro: Beginner Piano Lessons For Kids*. I know firsthand the joy of learning to play an instrument, and I want to share that joy with young, aspiring musicians. With this book, I aim to make it easy for kids to get started on their musical journey, explore their creativity, and unlock their full potential.

As a child, I was so passionate about music that I spent countless hours practicing my guitar and piano skills. Every spare moment was an opportunity to strum the strings or tinker with the keys. As I dedicated myself to my craft, I began to reap the rewards of my hard work. I could play more challenging pieces, express myself more deeply through music, and share my love for this art form with others. With dedication and perseverance, anyone can achieve their musical goals and discover the immense joy that music brings to our lives.

Learning a new instrument can be a daunting task, especially for beginners. I remember feeling overwhelmed when I first started, trying to make sense of sheet music, musical notation, and proper technique. That's why I wrote this book. I wanted to provide young, aspiring musicians with a resource to help them overcome those initial hurdles and build a solid foundation for their musical skills. With this book, I hope to inspire a new generation of pianists and make the journey of learning music more straightforward and more enjoyable.

Music has always held a special place in my heart; from a young age, I was drawn to its power to evoke emotions and tell stories. This deep-seated passion fueled my desire to learn new instruments and explore the endless possibilities of music. I picked up the guitar at just eight years old and dedicated myself to mastering it. Eventually, this journey led me to discover the magic of the piano. Anyone driven by a burning desire to learn music can unlock their full potential and achieve their dreams.

If you're reading this, you're likely a parent or guardian who recognizes a spark of passion and desire in your child for music. Maybe you've noticed them talking about wanting to learn the piano, or perhaps you've observed them tapping their feet or humming along to their favorite tunes. As someone who's been on a similar musical journey, I encourage you to nurture that spark and support your child's musical aspirations. Learning to play an instrument is a gift that will last a lifetime and can unlock creativity, boost confidence, and provide a lifelong source of joy. Let's inspire the next generation of musicians and help them unlock their full potential.

Little Maestro is more than just a book—it's a complete guide to help your child unlock their musical potential. It's designed to be easy to understand, with clear instructions, exercises, and practice songs that are tailored specifically to young learners. The lessons are structured in a way that allows children to progress at their own pace, starting from the basics and gradually working their way up to more complex pieces. With *Little Maestro* as their guide, your child can build confidence, develop new skills, and cultivate a lifelong love of music. Let's help them embark on a musical journey that will enrich their lives in so many ways.

This book is not just a set of piano lessons—it's an exciting journey of musical exploration that your child will cherish for years to come. Each chapter of the book builds upon the last, introducing new concepts, techniques, and pieces of music that will help your child become a well-rounded pianist. They will start with the basics of reading sheet music and understanding musical notation, then progress to playing simple melodies and chords. Along the way, they'll discover the rich history of music, learn about famous composers and their masterpieces, and explore fascinating facts about musical instruments. With *Little Maestro*, your child can immerse themselves in the world of music and uncover their own unique musical voice.

Little Maestro is not like any other piano lesson book out there—it stands out because of its focus on fostering creativity. While it's crucial to develop the fundamental skills of playing the piano, it's equally important to encourage kids to have fun and express their creativity through music. This book goes beyond just teaching the technical aspects of playing the piano—it includes a range of exercises and activities that inspire kids to explore their own unique musical style and make music their own. With *Little Maestro*, your child can learn the joy of creating music and discover their own unique voice on the piano.

Through my years of studying and playing music, I have gained a deep understanding of what it takes to master an instrument. However, I also know that it's essential to make music both fun and accessible, especially for young learners. That's why I've written *Little Maestro* in a way that's lively, positive, and easy to comprehend. This book is not just about teaching kids how to play the piano—it's about inspiring a love of music and encouraging them to enjoy the learning process. With *Little Maestro*, your child can experience the joy of making music while building essential skills that will last a lifetime.

By the end of the book, your child will have developed a strong foundation for their piano skills and be on their way to becoming a true piano virtuoso. *Little Maestro* is the perfect book for any young aspiring musician.

So if you're looking for a way to help your child develop their musical skills, build their confidence, and have fun, *Little Maestro* is the perfect book for you.

Let's make beautiful music together!

CHAPTER 1:

So You Wanna Play the Piano...

Beginner Piano Lessons for Kids

Taylor Kent W.

Cool Fact #1: The piano is over 300 years old! Did you know that the piano has existed for over 300 years? It's like a musical time machine! Back in the year 1700, a clever inventor named Bartolomeo Cristofori from Italy created this incredible instrument.

Before the piano, people played other keyboard instruments, but the piano was super special. It could make soft and loud sounds, just like magic! How? Well, inside the piano, there are little hammers that hit the strings when we press the keys. This lets us control how loud or soft the music can be. It's like having a volume knob for your songs!

So, when you sit down at the piano, remember that you're joining a musical tradition that's been going on for more than 300 years. Let your fingers dance on the keys, and let the music take you to amazing places. Get ready to make beautiful melodies and have the time of your life!

Are you ready to embark on a musical journey that will take you to new heights of creativity, expression, and joy? Well, if you're holding this book in your hands, then I feel you are!

The piano is a remarkable instrument that has captivated audiences for centuries. Its versatility allows it to be played in any genre of music, from classical to pop, jazz to rock. Whether you're looking to play a soulful ballad, a lively polka, or a powerful concerto, the piano can bring your musical vision to life.

As a piano player myself, there's nothing quite like the feeling of sitting down at the keys and letting your fingers dance across the notes. It's a feeling of freedom, of creativity, of pure bliss. And the best part? Anyone can learn how to play the piano, regardless of age, experience, or musical background.

In this chapter, we'll be exploring the basics of piano playing. We'll talk about the history of the instrument, its parts, and its components. Whether you're a complete newbie or have some prior experience with music, this chapter will set you up for success as you begin your piano-playing journey. So, let's dive in and discover the magic of the piano!

WHY PLAY THE PIANO?

Playing the piano is more than just making beautiful music—it can also help you in many other areas of your life! When you learn to play the piano, you'll develop skills like self-discipline, focus, and timing. You'll also learn how to handle stress and improve your memory. These valuable skills will help you in school, sports, and other activities.

Playing the piano is also a great way to express emotions and develop creativity. You'll be able to create your own music and play your favorite songs, which is a lot of fun! Plus, when you play the piano, you'll learn how to listen carefully to music and develop a better ear for different sounds.

Not only that but playing the piano can help you develop a love for music that will last a lifetime. You'll appreciate all kinds of music and be able to play for your family and friends. So, let's look at more of the wonderful benefits of learning to play the piano!

Teaches Discipline

Playing the piano can also help you learn the valuable skill of discipline. Discipline means doing things even when you don't feel like it or when they are hard. When you practice the piano regularly, even on days when you don't feel like it, you are training yourself to be disciplined. This skill can help you in many other areas of life, like doing homework or studying for tests. So, if you want to become better at staying focused and getting things done, playing the piano can help you do just that!

Builds Self-Esteem

Playing the piano is a great way to build self-esteem! When you learn to play a new piece of music or master a difficult song, it feels really good! You will feel proud of yourself and more confident in your abilities. Plus, when you perform for others or play in a recital, you get to share your amazing talent with others and show off all your hard work. This will give you a huge boost of self-esteem and make you feel great about yourself.

Helps Improve Memory and Improves Brain Development

Playing the piano is not only fun, but it can also help your brain get stronger! When you play the piano, you must remember many things—like how to read the notes and which keys to press. This helps your memory get better, just like how exercising your body makes your muscles stronger.

Playing the piano can also help your brain develop in other ways. It requires a lot of mental focus and concentration, which can help you get better at paying attention and staying focused on tasks. Plus, the coordination required to play different notes with each hand at the same time can help other parts of your brain work together better.

So not only will playing the piano help you make wonderful music, but it can also help your brain become stronger and more capable!

Better Performance at School

Playing the piano can help you become a better student! When you practice playing the piano, you are also practicing skills that can help you do better in school. For example, playing the piano can help improve your concentration and focus, which can make it easier for you to pay attention in class and remember important information. It can also help you become better at problem-solving and critical thinking, which are essential skills in many subjects like math and science. Plus, playing the piano can be a great stress reliever, which can help you feel more relaxed and focused when you need to study or take a test.

Social Skills

Playing the piano can also help you learn social skills! When you take piano lessons or play music with others, you have the opportunity to work as part of a team. You can learn how to communicate with others, take turns, and share ideas. Playing music together can also be a lot of fun and can help you make new friends! And when you perform in front of others, you can develop confidence and learn how to handle nerves and stage fright. All of these skills will be helpful to you in many areas of your life, both now and in the future.

WHY THE PIANO IS A FANTASTIC FIRST INSTRUMENT

There are many reasons why the piano makes a great first instrument. Let's dive into some of them!

Sounds Good

One of the best things about the piano is that it sounds great right from the start. When you press a key, it makes a clear and beautiful sound. This means that even as a beginner, you can start playing simple melodies and feel like you're making real music. You don't have to worry about sounding squeaky or screechy like some other instruments can sound when played by a beginner.

Provides a Solid Foundation

Learning to play the piano provides a solid foundation for learning other instruments later on. Piano playing involves reading sheet music, playing with both hands, and understanding musical concepts like rhythm and timing. These skills can translate to other instruments, such as guitar or violin. Plus, learning how to read sheet music and understand the basics of music theory makes learning any other instrument much easier.

Improves Coordination

Playing the piano involves using both hands independently of each other, which can be tricky at first but ultimately improves your coordination. You'll also be using your feet to control the pedals, which adds another level of complexity to your playing. As you practice, you'll develop greater hand-eye coordination, dexterity, and control.

Overall, learning to play the piano is an excellent choice for a first instrument. It sounds great right from the start, provides a solid foundation for learning other instruments later on, and improves your coordination. So, grab a piano and start exploring the world of music!

BASIC REQUIREMENTS FOR PLAYING THE PIANO

Are you ready to learn about the basic requirements for playing the piano? It's essential to have some basic skills and traits to make learning to play the piano a fun and successful experience. Let's explore the three main things you need to get started on your piano journey!

Size of Hand

To play the piano, you need to have hands that are big enough to reach the keys comfortably. This means that you can stretch out your fingers to play the keys without feeling uncomfortable or straining your fingers. However, don't worry if your hands are still small—as you grow older, your hands will get bigger and stronger, and you will be able to reach the keys more easily.

Finger Independence

Another important skill you need to have to play the piano is finger independence. This means that your fingers can move independently from each other without getting mixed up or stuck. With finger independence, you can play different notes with different fingers and make beautiful music!

A Desire to Learn

The most vital thing you need to have to play the piano is a desire to learn! Learning the piano takes time and practice, but it's worth it in the end. If you're willing to put in the effort and have fun along the way, you'll be amazed at what you can accomplish.

FOR THE PARENTS (OR GUARDIANS)

Before your child begins piano lessons, there are a few things you should consider as a parent to ensure their success. By following these tips, you can set your child up for a positive and enjoyable experience with music.

Finding the Right Teacher

If you are looking for more hands-on instruction for your child, finding the right piano teacher is essential for their success. Look for a teacher with experience working with children and a friendly and encouraging teaching style. A good teacher will help your child develop good habits and make learning the piano fun.

Get the Right Equipment

To help your child succeed in piano lessons, make sure they have access to the right equipment. This includes a quality piano or keyboard and a comfortable bench or chair. Ensure the piano is tuned regularly to help your child develop an ear for good pitch.

Create a Practice Space

Create a designated practice space for your child, free from distractions and with good lighting. This space should be inviting and comfortable, making it easy for your child to focus on their practice.

Establish a Routine

Establish a regular practice routine that works for your child and fits into their schedule. Consistency is key, and regular practice will help your child progress quickly and build confidence.

Set Goals

Setting achievable goals is an excellent way to help your child stay motivated and track their progress. Encourage your child to set short-term and long-term goals and celebrate their achievements along the way.

Encourage Creativity

Music is a form of creative expression, and piano lessons should be a fun and creative experience for your child. Encourage your child to experiment with different sounds and rhythms and allow them to express themselves through their playing.

Be Patient

Learning the piano takes time and patience. Encourage your child to take their time and not to become discouraged if progress seems slow. With regular practice and patience, your child will develop the skills they need to play beautiful music.

Be Supportive

As a parent, your support and encouragement can make a huge difference in your child's progress. Attend their recitals, listen to them practice, and offer positive feedback and praise. Celebrating each success, no matter how small, is a recipe for confidence and encouragement.

Make It Fun

Learning the piano should be a fun and enjoyable experience for your child. Encourage them to experiment with different styles of music and play songs they love. The more fun they have, the more likely they are to stick with it and develop a lifelong love of music.

Stay Involved

Stay involved in your child's musical journey. Keep in touch with their teacher, attend their recitals and performances, and continue encouraging them to explore their musical abilities. With your support, your child can develop a love of music that will last a lifetime.

WHEN/IF YOUR CHILD SHOULD TAKE PIANO LESSONS

As a parent, you want to give your child every opportunity to learn and grow. One great way to do this is by enrolling them in piano lessons. Piano lessons can provide numerous benefits for children, from developing musical skills to building confidence and discipline. But when is the right time to start lessons? And how do you know if your child is ready? In this section, we will discuss when you should consider getting your child piano lessons.

When to Consider Piano Lessons

If your child shows an interest in music, enjoys listening to and playing music, or has expressed an interest in learning to play the piano, it may be time to consider piano lessons. Children as young as four or five can start taking piano lessons, although the ideal age varies depending on the child's maturity and readiness to learn. It's a good idea to find a qualified and experienced piano teacher who can work with your child's individual needs and interests.

WHAT DID WE LEARN?

Let's take a moment to think about what we learned by reading this chapter!

- What are some basic requirements for playing the piano?
- Why is the piano a great first instrument?
- What are some benefits of playing the piano besides learning how to make awesome music?

Wow! You've finished a chapter! That means you've earned your very first gold star! Each time you finish a chapter of this book, you will see this image to let you know you're doing an awesome job!

Congratulations! You've taken your first steps on your journey to becoming a pianist! In this chapter, we learned about the wonderful world of playing the piano. We talked about how playing the piano can be a fun and rewarding experience and how it can help you develop valuable skills like discipline, memory, and coordination. We also learned about the basic requirements for playing the piano, including the size of your hand, finger independence, and the most important thing—a desire to learn!

In the next chapter, we're going to start working on some techniques that will help you become an even better piano player. We'll be exploring the proper way to sit at the piano, the different parts of the piano, and how to position your fingers on the keys. So get ready to put your fingers to the keys and let's start making beautiful music together!

CHAPTER 2:

Let's Start With the Basics

Beginner Piano Lessons for Kids

Taylor Kent W.

Cool Fact #2: Did you know that piano keys were first made from wood (Jackon, 2021)?
Yep, you heard it right; WOOD! It's like playing music on mini tree branches!

In the olden days, when the piano was just starting its musical journey, talented craftsmen carefully carved each key out of wood. They made sure each key was smooth and just the right size for our little fingers to press.

As time passed, piano makers started using other materials like ivory and plastic to make the keys. But the memory of those wooden keys remains, reminding us of the piano's early days.

So, let the magic of wooden piano keys inspire you to play beautiful melodies and create your own musical story. Who knows, maybe one day you'll play a song that will make people say, "Wow, that sounds as amazing as a symphony of trees!" Keep playing and let your music shine!

Now that you know the basics, it's time to take things up a notch. In this chapter, we'll talk about posture positions and how to position your hands correctly on the keys. You'll also learn about different playing techniques to make your playing sound more polished and professional. So, let's dive in and start playing like a pro!

POSITION AND POSTURE MATTER

Having the proper position and posture is critical to play the piano correctly and avoiding injuries. This section will teach you how to sit correctly at the piano, where to place your hands, and other essential techniques to make your piano-playing experience enjoyable and comfortable. So let's get started!

What Is Posture?

Posture is how you hold your body when you sit or stand. It's recommended to have good posture because it helps you play the piano better and can prevent you from getting tired or sore. When you have good posture, your body is in the right position to play the piano without hurting yourself or making mistakes. So, always try to sit up straight and keep your feet flat on the floor when playing the piano.

Bench or Seat Position

When you sit down to play the piano, it's essential to make sure you're sitting in the right position. The bench or seat you're sitting on should be at a height where your feet can rest flat on the ground. Your knees should be at a right angle, and your back should be straight. Make sure to sit up tall, and don't slouch! This will help you play the piano with better posture and avoid hurting your back or neck. Look at the image below for an example of slouching!

Position of Your Arms and the Height of the Piano Seat

It's also important to have the correct arm position and to adjust the height of the piano seat. Your arms should be relaxed, and your elbows should be level with the keys. This means that you may need to adjust the height of your piano seat so that your arms and elbows are in the right position. If your seat is too low or too high, it can cause strain on your arms, shoulders, and back, making it difficult to play. So, make sure to adjust your seat to the correct height so you can play comfortably and correctly!

How to Change the Bench Height

Adjusting the height of your piano bench helps maintain proper posture and prevent strain on your arms and back. Here are a few ways to do it:

- **Use books or pillows:** If your bench is too low, you can try placing some thick books or a pillow on top of the seat to raise it up.
- **Adjust the legs:** Some piano benches have adjustable legs that can be raised or lowered to change the height. Check to see if your bench has this feature.
- **Get a new bench:** If all else fails, consider getting a new bench that is adjustable or already at the right height for you.

Remember, it's vital to have the right bench height so you can play comfortably and avoid injury.

Feet Flat on the Ground

When you sit at the piano, make sure your feet don't dangle! Dangling feet can make it difficult to maintain good posture, and you might not be able to reach the pedals. Instead, you can use a footstool to make sure your feet are flat on the ground. This way, you can keep your back straight and comfortable while you play the piano.

Correct Body Position/Posture

Body position/posture is how you hold your body when you play the piano. It's important to sit up straight with your shoulders relaxed and your feet flat on the ground. Your arms should be loose, and your elbows at your sides. This helps you play more comfortably and with better technique. Remember, good posture is key to becoming a great pianist!

The Perfect Key Technique

The perfect key technique is an essential aspect of playing the piano. This technique is all about keeping your fingers curved and relaxed and striking the keys with the tips of your fingers. This helps to produce a clear and accurate sound. Remember to keep your hands and fingers relaxed and avoid hitting the keys too hard or too softly. Practicing this technique will help you become a better pianist over time!

Posture and position matter a lot when playing the piano! Remember to sit up straight, keep your feet flat on the ground and keep your arms and hands in the correct position. Make sure you are at the right height and not too far or too close to the piano. All of these things will help you play the piano better and avoid any pain or discomfort. Keep practicing your posture and position, and soon you will become a pro at it!

HAND TECHNIQUES

Now that we have learned about the importance of posture and position, it's time to focus on how you use your hands when playing the piano. In this section, we'll explore some techniques that will help you become a better piano player. Let's get started!

Relaxed and Curved Fingers

It's good practice to keep your fingers curved and relaxed when playing the piano. This means that you shouldn't flatten them out or tense them up. Instead, your fingers should be in a gentle curve, almost like they're holding a small ball. This way, you can play the keys smoothly and with ease. Remember to keep your hands and fingers relaxed throughout your playing!

Straight but Relaxed Thumbs

When you play the piano, it's vital to keep your thumbs straight but also relaxed. This helps your fingers move smoothly and quickly between the keys. If your thumbs are too stiff or bent, it can make it harder to play the right notes. Remember to keep them straight and loose!

Don't Buckle Your Fingers

It's important to avoid buckling your fingers when you are playing. This means that your fingers should not collapse and touch the keys with their sides. Instead, keep your fingers curved and use the tips of your fingers to hit the keys. This will help you play more accurately and prevent injury. Remember to keep your fingers relaxed as well!

Use the Weight of Your Arms

Using the weight of your arms to press the keys is good practice when you play. That means letting your arms be loose and heavy like they're hanging from your shoulders. Don't try to press the keys with just your fingers or hands, as this can make your hands feel tired and can even cause pain over time. Instead, try to relax and let the weight of your arms do the work.

Keep Your Wrists Flexible

Whenever you are playing the piano, it's essential to keep your wrists flexible. This means you don't want your wrists to be too stiff or too floppy. You should try to keep your wrists straight but not locked. It's like you're gently holding a ball in your hand, and your wrist can move freely around it. This will help you play the keys more easily and with better control. If your wrists are too stiff or too floppy, it can make playing the piano harder and may even cause discomfort or pain. So remember to keep your wrists flexible!

Use the Tip of Your Pinky Finger

When you play the piano, it's helpful to use the tip of your pinky finger! This will help you to press each key accurately and with control. When your finger is at the tip, it has more strength and precision than if it's flat on the key. It might take some practice, but with time, you'll be a pro at using the tip of your pinky!

In this section, we learned about hand techniques that are important to remember while playing the piano. Keeping our fingers curved and relaxed, thumbs straight but relaxed, not buckling our fingers, using the weight of our arms to press the keys, keeping our wrists flexible, and using the tip of our pinky are some of the techniques that can help us become better piano players. Using these techniques, we can avoid strain on our hands and play the piano more effectively.

ACTIVITY TIME: THE HAND CAVE

Let's look at some fun activities to help improve our piano playing technique!

The Hand Cave

Do you want to improve your piano playing technique? Here's a fun idea that might help!

First, let's talk about the thumb. It's a special finger that doesn't press the keys like the others. But if it's not in the right position, it can cause problems for the rest of your hand.

That's where the hand cave comes in. Imagine that your hand can create a little cave for some small critters to take shelter. With wrists straight, place the base of your palm on a desk or table. Let's call it the heel of the palm. With the heel of the palm touching the table, curve your fingers and thumb to make a little cave and entryway to the cave. It should look roughly like the next picture. The most important thing here is to keep the hand released, curved, and wrists straight. Your fingers should create a relaxed curve with your fingertips touching the desk, creating a little bubble or cave. Remembering the "Hand Cave," you won't forget the right posture.

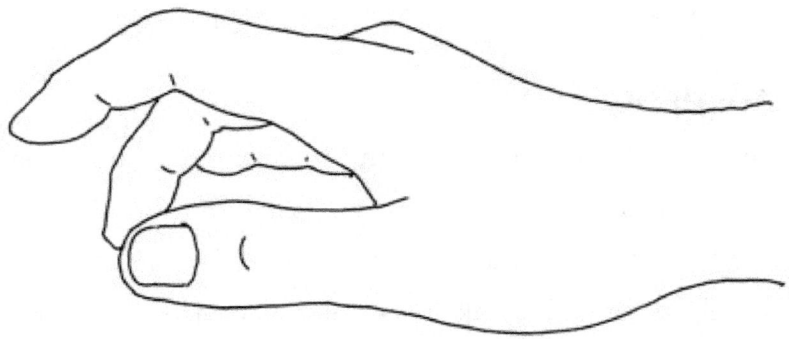

The Kitten

Let's pretend that every time you sit down to play the piano, there's a cute, furry kitten sitting on top of your piano keys. When you play the piano, you need to be very gentle and careful not to disturb the kitten. So, instead of pushing down on the keys with your fingers, imagine that you're petting the kitten with the tips of your fingers. Keep your fingers relaxed and curved as you stroke the kitten's fur. This will help you keep a good hand position and prevent your fingers from buckling. And who knows, maybe you'll even make a new furry friend!

Not-So-Scary Spider

Are you ready to warm up your hands like a spider doing yoga? First, place your hands on a table with your fingers nicely curved and your wrists resting on the surface. This is your spider shape! Imagine that your spider needs to stretch each of its legs.

Start by reaching one finger at a time upward, starting with your thumb. Make sure to keep your other fingertips touching the table and don't let your knuckles collapse. You can even try to touch something above your hand, like a toy or a book. This gives your spider something to aim for!

At first, your 3rd and 4th fingers may move together. That's okay! Keep practicing and try to move your 4 fingers independently. Once you've got it down, you can do specific exercises for each of your spider's legs. You can write out finger numbers in random order and lift the spider legs accordingly. For example, you can lift your 1st, 3rd, 5th, 2nd, and 4th fingers in that order. Keep practicing and your spider will become stretchier and stronger!

ACTIVITY TIME: STRENGTHEN YOUR FINGERS!

Now it's time to practice these awesome activities to improve your finger strength!

Your Fingers Are Thirsty!

Get ready to quench your fingers' thirst with this fun exercise! Start by placing your hands flat on a table, palms facing up. Imagine your fingers are hot and need a refreshing drink. Your thumb is the drink waiter and will bring water to each finger. One at a time, your fingers will lift up and meet your thumb to get their drink. They will touch each other for a moment before going back down to the table. You can lift your other fingers a little if needed. Let's have some fun and make cool sound effects like "Slurp slurp slurp... Mmm!" when we touch our fingers to our thumbs, just like we're sipping a delicious drink. This exercise will help make our fingers strong and flexible!

Silly Mini Sit-Ups

Let's warm up and strengthen your hands and arms with some silly mini sit-ups! Start by placing your hands on a flat surface with your fingers stretched out. Then, say "Sil-ly sit-ups" while doing the following:

1. Bend your fingers to make a fist.
2. Straighten your fingers to open your hand.
3. Turn your hands over so your palms touch the flat surface.
4. Turn your hands back over so the backs of your hands touch the flat surface again.

Keep repeating this movement, and try to go faster each time!

WHAT DID WE LEARN?

- What is the correct hand position in piano playing?
- What is the purpose of using silly hand shapes like a cave when playing the piano?
- Can you explain how to make a cave or a spider shape with your hands and why it helps with hand positioning?
- What is the importance of avoiding hand position problems in piano playing?
- How does the Spider exercise help in improving finger control and independence?

- What is the "Thirsty Fingers" exercise, and how does it help warm up the fingers and improve coordination?
- How does the "Silly Mini Sit-Ups" exercise help warm up the palms of the hands and forearms while encouraging bilateral coordination?

Another chapter finished? Wow! You're flying! Here's your second gold star! You're doing a fantastic job!

Great job! You just learned some fun exercises to help you get better at playing the piano. By pretending to pet kittens and stretching like a spider, you can improve your finger control and technique.

Now, it's time to move on to the next step—playing on the actual keys! In the next chapter, you'll learn how to play specific notes on the piano and how to read sheet music. Get ready to start playing some cool tunes!

CHAPTER 3:

Moving onto the Keys!

Beginner Piano Lessons for Kids

Taylor Kent W.

Cool Fact #3: The most expensive piano ever sold was bought for $3.22 million!

Have you ever heard of the Heintzman Crystal Piano? This piano is like no other. It's not just any ordinary piano—it's a true masterpiece! This special piano is made entirely out of crystal, making it sparkle and shine like a dazzling gem.

Now, imagine this incredible piano being played by one of the most famous pianists in the whole wide world at the Beijing Olympic Games. Can you picture it? The entire audience was mesmerized by the beautiful music filling the air as the pianist's fingers danced across the crystal keys. It was like a magical moment frozen in time!

So, keep playing, keep dreaming, and remember that the true value of music comes from your heart and the joy it brings. Your music is priceless, my friend!

In this chapter, we will explore the piano keys and their positions. By the end of this chapter, you'll be able to find your way around the keyboard like a pro. Get ready to make friends with the keys!

START WITH MIDDLE C

In this section, we will begin by exploring the very first note you'll learn on the piano—middle C! You'll discover where middle C is located on the keyboard and how to play it with both your left and right hand. So let's get started!

What Is Middle C?

Middle C is a special key on the piano. This will be an essential key to remember, as it is a necessary reference for reading sheet music. It is called "middle" because it's the middlemost C key on the keyboard. Middle C is a significant key to learn because it will help you find your way around the rest of the piano.

What's the Big Deal About Middle C?

Middle C is so important because it is a reference point on the piano. It helps you find your way around the keyboard and understand where the other notes are located. When you start playing songs, you'll often begin with middle C, and many pieces of music use it as a guide to help you figure out which keys to play next. Think of finding middle C as like finding North when reading a map. It's going to be a special landmark for you to easily feel where your fingers are on the keys while you play.

How to Find Middle C

To locate middle C on a piano, follow these steps:

1. Look for the group of two black keys in the middle of the piano.
2. Find the white key directly to the left of the group of two black keys.
3. Congratulations! You have found middle C! It's the white key in the center of the piano, just to the left of the group of two black keys.
4. Once you have found middle C, try playing it with your finger. You can play it by pressing down on the key with your finger, just like you would press a button.

Remember, middle C is an important key to know because it's the starting point for many songs and melodies.

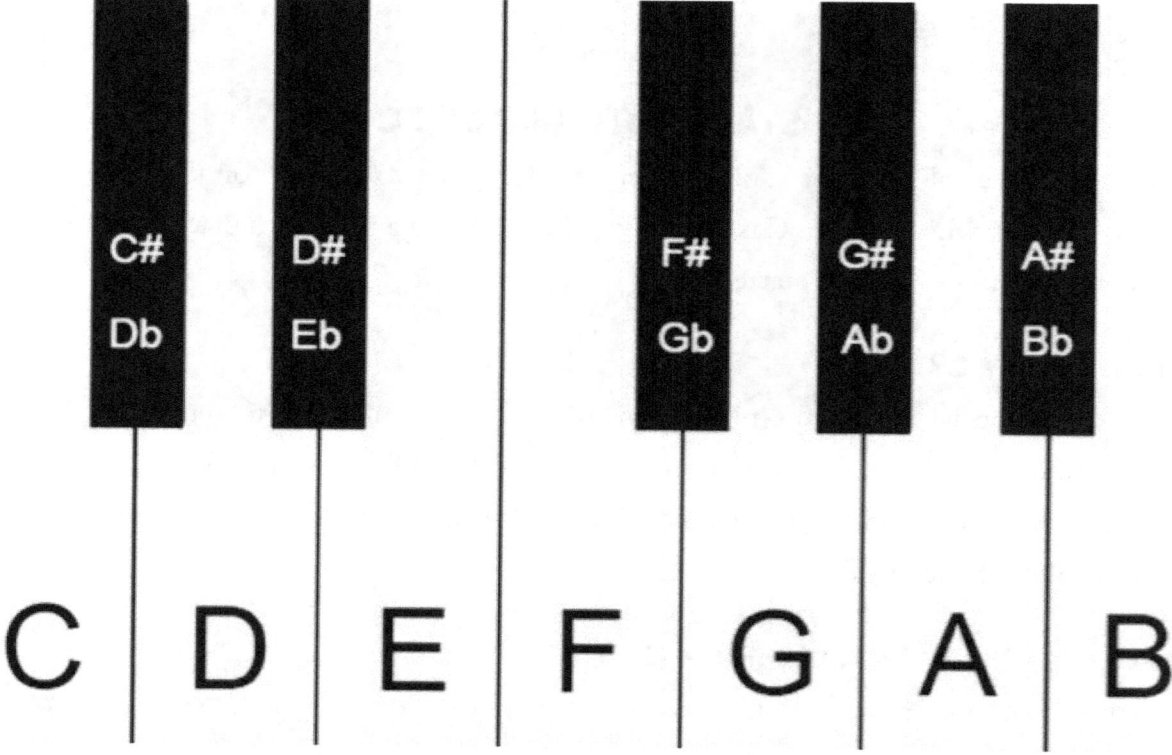

Finger Positioning for Middle C

Knowing the correct finger position for middle C is very important.

To start, let's put our right hand on the keyboard. Find the group of two black keys closest to the middle of the keyboard. Now, look to the left of those black keys. Do you see a white key just to the left of the first black key? That's middle C!

To play middle C, place your right thumb (that's the finger on the side of your hand closest to your pointer finger) on middle C. Your other four fingers should rest comfortably on the four white keys to the right of middle C, like little hills.

Remember to keep your hand curved and relaxed and to press down each key gently but firmly with the tip of your finger. Congratulations, you've found middle C and are ready to play your first note on the piano!

In this section, we learned about the importance of middle C on the piano and how to locate it. We also learned about the correct finger position to play middle C. With this knowledge, you can start playing simple melodies on the piano using middle C as your starting point.

LET'S TALK ABOUT THE OTHER GUYS!

You may have noticed that some keys are black and some are white. Do you know why? In this section, we'll explore why pianos have black and white keys and how many of each there are. We'll also learn the names of the seven white keys. Get ready to become a piano key expert!

Why Are There Black and White Keys?

The reason why a piano has both black and white keys is because the black keys represent the sharps and flats. In music, a sharp raises the pitch of a note, and a flat lowers the pitch of a note (Ross, n.d.). The white keys represent the natural notes of the musical scale, such as A, B, C, D, E, F, and G. The combination of the white and black keys helps musicians create different sounds and play a wide range of music. The black keys also act as a visual guide to help musicians easily find and play the sharps and flats of the notes. So, the black and white keys work together to make beautiful melodies and harmonies!

How Many of Each Type of Key Are There?

There are a variety of different pianos. Some have more keys than others. On an 88-key piano, there are 52 white keys and 36 black keys (Ross, n.d.). The white keys are all touching at the bottom of the keyboard, while the black keys separate them at the top of the key in groups of twos and threes. For a single octave, there are seven white keys and five black keys (Ross, n.d). On an 88-key piano, this creates about seven full octaves!

The Names of the Seven White Keys

The white keys on the piano are named after the first seven letters of the alphabet: A, B, C, D, E, F, and G.

One fun way to remember these letters is by using acronyms instead of just the alphabet. Here are a few examples:

- **A**ll **B**eautiful **C**hildren **D**o **E**njoy **F**airy Tales and **G**ames
- **A**lways **B**e **C**ourageous, **D**on't **E**ver **F**ear **G**reatness
- **A**pples **B**ring **C**runchy **D**elicious **E**ating **F**un and **G**oodness

Now, let's learn how to find each of these white keys on the piano.

- **A:** Find the group of three black keys. The white key to the left of the rightmost black key is A.
- **B:** Find the group of three black keys. The white key to the right of the rightmost black key is B.
- **C:** The white key to the left of the pair of two black keys.
- **D:** The white key between the pair of two black keys.
- **E:** The white key to the right of the pair of two black keys.
- **F:** The white key directly to the left of the three black keys.
- G: Find the group of three black keys; the white key to the right of the left-most black key is G.

It's good to remember that a flat note means that it is a lower note and will be the black key to the left of the note, while a sharp note is a higher note and will be the black key to the right. For example, Ab will be the black key to the left of A, while A# will be the black key to the right of A (*Music for kids: piano playing basics,* n.d.).

In this section, we learned the difference between black and white keys on a piano and why they are important. We also discovered how many black and white keys there are on a standard piano. Lastly, we learned the names of the seven white keys and some fun acronyms to help remember them. Understanding these concepts is essential for playing and reading music on the piano. Once you know the names of the keys and where to find them, you're well on your way to playing some of your most favorite tunes!

PIANO FINGERING

Welcome to the next section of our piano lesson, where we will learn all about "Piano Fingering." Fingering is an essential part of playing the piano, and it involves using the right fingers to play the right keys. In this section, we'll explore how to position your fingers and hands on the piano keys to play beautiful melodies and songs. Let's get playing!

Numbering Your Fingers

When you play the piano, it's crucial to use the correct fingers on each key. To do this, we use numbers to name each finger. The thumb is number 1, the index finger is number 2, the middle finger is number 3, the ring finger is number 4, and the pinky finger is number 5. You can practice numbering your fingers by holding your hand up and naming each finger, starting with the thumb and counting all the way to the pinky. With practice, you'll be able to quickly and easily identify each finger by its number!

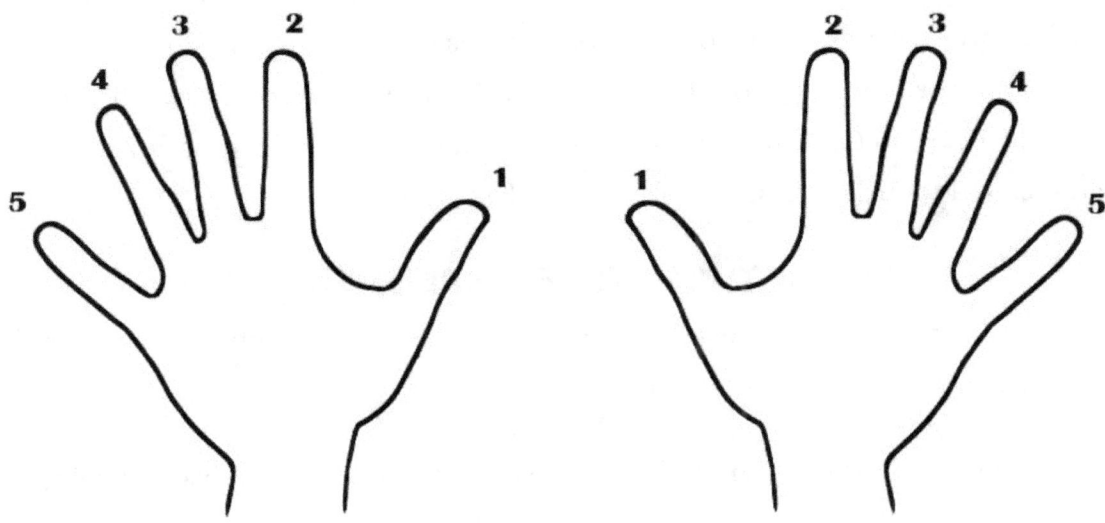

Where Do You Place Your Right Hand?

When you play the piano, your hands have a specific place to go. Your right hand starts on the right side of the middle C and plays the white keys to the right of it. So, your thumb (#1) starts on the C key, then moves on to play D with your index finger (#2), E with your middle finger (#3), F with your ring finger (#4), and G with your pinky finger (#5). It's important to keep your fingers curved and your wrist relaxed. This will help you move your fingers smoothly and make beautiful music!

Where Do You Place Your Left Hand?

Each keyboard is different but for this example, let's say the lowest key on your keyboard is A. When you place your left hand on the keyboard, your pinky finger should be on the lowest white key, which is called "A." Your ring finger should be on the next white key to the right, which is called "B." Your middle finger should be on the next white key to the right, which is called "C." Your index finger should be on the next white key to the right, which is called "D." Finally, your thumb should be on the next white key to the right, which is called "E." Of course, this may differ depending on the song you are playing, but this is a great place to start!

In this section, we learned about piano fingering and how to number our fingers. We also learned about the proper placement of our hands on the piano keys. For the right hand, we place our thumb on middle C and our other fingers on the white keys to the right, while for the left hand, our pinky finger should be on the lowest white key, and our remaining fingers should rest on the white keys to the right of our pinky finger. Again, this is where we start for learning but not necessarily where we start for each song. If this is too much of a stretch for your arms, feel free to place the pinky on the C key one octave down from middle C and the other fingers on the keys D, E, F and G, with your thumb on G. Remember to keep your fingers curved, and your hand relaxed to make it easier to play piano like a pro!

ACTIVITY TIME: THREESIES!

"Threesies" is a fun game to help you learn how to use the first three fingers of your right hand (thumb, index, and third finger) as a group.

To play threesies, let's start by sitting at the piano with good posture, your back straight, and your feet on the floor.

Now, let's take a look at the keyboard. Do you see the group of three black keys on the piano? We're going to use the white keys next to these black keys to play the game.

Place your right-hand thumb on the first white key to the left of the group of three black keys, the F key. Your index finger will go on the key to the right of your thumb, the G key, and your third finger will go on the key to the right of your index finger, the A key.

Now, we're going to play the keys from left to right: first, your thumb, then your index, then the third finger.

Let's do it again! Start with your thumb on the F key, then play the index finger, then the third finger.

Keep playing this pattern of threesies (thumb, index, third finger) over and over. Try to keep a steady pace, and make sure you're pressing the keys firmly.

As you practice threesies, you will start to get more comfortable using the first three fingers of your right hand. Remember, your thumb is shorter than the other fingers, so it needs to sit on the white keys in a different way. It might take a few weeks or even months to get used to it, but don't worry. Keep practicing and have fun with threesies!

ACTIVITY TIME: RACE TO MIDDLE C!

Here's an activity that you can play to help you learn how to identify notes on the piano keyboard! It's called "The Race to Middle C." All you need is a piano or keyboard, two game pieces like coins or buttons, and some letter cards with notes on them (like A, B, C, etc.).

Here's how to play:

1. You and your teacher or friend place your game pieces at opposite ends of the keyboard.
2. Take turns drawing a card with a note on it, and then move your game piece to that note on the keyboard. For example, if you draw a card with the note "A#," you would move your game piece to the nearest "A#" key on the keyboard.
3. The first person to reach middle C wins!

This game is great for practicing note identification on the piano keyboard. You can also make it more challenging by using notated flash cards with notes on the staff instead of just letter cards. Or you can race from one end of the keyboard to the other to make the game last longer.

Sometimes, you can also change the direction that your game piece moves depending on whether you draw a sharp or flat note. This will help you understand the concept of raising sharps and lowering flats on the keyboard.

Playing games is a fun and effective way to learn how to play the piano, and this game is sure to help you improve your note-identification skills!

What Did We Learn?

Let's take a peek at what we have learned in this chapter:

- Why does the piano have black and white keys?
- Where do you place your left hand on the piano?
- How do you number fingers on your hands?
- Where do you place your right hand on the piano?
- How many white keys are there on a piano?

Guess what? You've completed another chapter! Way to go! You know what that means? Another gold star! Well done!

In this chapter, we learned the basics of playing the piano. We learned about the different parts of the piano, how to sit correctly at the piano, and where to place our hands. We also learned about the black and white keys and the names of the seven white keys. Finally, we played some fun games to help us practice what we learned.

Now, it's time to move on to another important aspect of playing the piano: reading music! In the next chapter, we will learn about the ABCs of reading music. We will explore the different symbols used in sheet music and learn how to read notes on the staff. Get ready to take your piano-playing skills to the next level!

CHAPTER 4:

The ABCs of Sheet Music

Beginner Piano Lessons for Kids

Taylor Kent W.

Cool Fact #5: To keep your piano sounding sweet, it will need to be tuned regularly!

Just like how you visit the doctor to stay healthy, pianos need a visit from a special person called a piano tuner. They have super sensitive ears and special tools to make sure every key on your piano sounds just right. They make tiny adjustments to the strings inside the piano to keep everything in tune.

Think of it as a musical massage for your piano. Each string is carefully stretched or relaxed, like a rubber band, until it produces the perfect pitch. It's like giving your piano a big hug and telling it, "You sound amazing!"

But here's the fun part: Getting your piano tuned can feel like a little adventure. You get to hear the different sounds as the tuner works their magic. It's like a musical puzzle, and you can watch as the tuner twists and turns those tuning pegs to create the perfect melody.

And guess what? Tuning your piano isn't a one-time thing. Just like how you brush your teeth every day to keep them sparkly clean, pianos need regular tuning too. With each passing season, changes in temperature and humidity can make the piano's strings wiggle a little. That's why it's important to have your piano tuned a few times a year, just to keep it sounding sweet.

So, the next time your piano tuner comes to visit, you can be their little helper. Listen carefully to the sounds they make and watch how they turn those magical pegs. And when they're done, you'll have a piano that sings with joy and fills your heart with beautiful music!

In this chapter, we will learn about the ABCs of reading music. Just like how you learn the ABCs to read words, we will learn the musical ABCs to read music. We'll keep it simple and easy for you to understand, so get ready to become a musical reader!

WHAT IS SHEET MUSIC?

Have you ever seen a piece of paper with dots and lines on it and wondered what it was? That's sheet music! Sheet music is a way for musicians to write down the notes they play, so others can read and play the same music too. In this section, we'll learn more about sheet music and how to read it.

Sheet music is a written or printed document that shows you how to play music on an instrument. It can be like a recipe that tells you what notes to play and how long to play them for.

Sheet music can have different symbols and markings that give instructions, such as how fast or slow to play, when to be louder or softer, and when to take a breath. It can also show you what the melody is, which is the main tune of the song, and what the harmony is, which is the accompaniment or background music.

Sheet music can come in different formats, such as books, loose sheets, or digital files. You can find sheet music for many different types of music, from classical music to pop songs.

For example, if you wanted to learn how to play a popular song on the piano, you could find the sheet music for that song and use it as a guide. Or, if you were in a band and wanted to learn a new song together, you could use the sheet music to make sure everyone was playing the right parts at the right times.

LEARNING MUSIC NOTATION

In this section, we will explore the basics of reading music notation. We will look at different symbols and signs that are used in sheet music and learn how to read them. By the end of this section, you will have a better understanding of how to read music and be on your way to playing your favorite songs on the piano!

The staff is a set of five lines and four spaces on which music is written. Think of it like a musical road map! Each line and space on the staff represents a different musical note (*Sheet music facts for kids,* n.d.).

When you look at sheet music, you'll see little dots and shapes on the staff. These are called notes. The placement of the notes on the staff tells you which note to play on your instrument.

Notes can be written on the lines or in the spaces between the lines. Each note has its own unique shape and position on the staff. For example, on the treble clef, a note called "G" is on the second line of the staff, while a note called "B" is on the third line of the staff.

It's important to remember that each line and space on the staff represents a different note, so it's important to pay attention to where the notes are placed on the staff.

Here's an example of what the staff looks like:

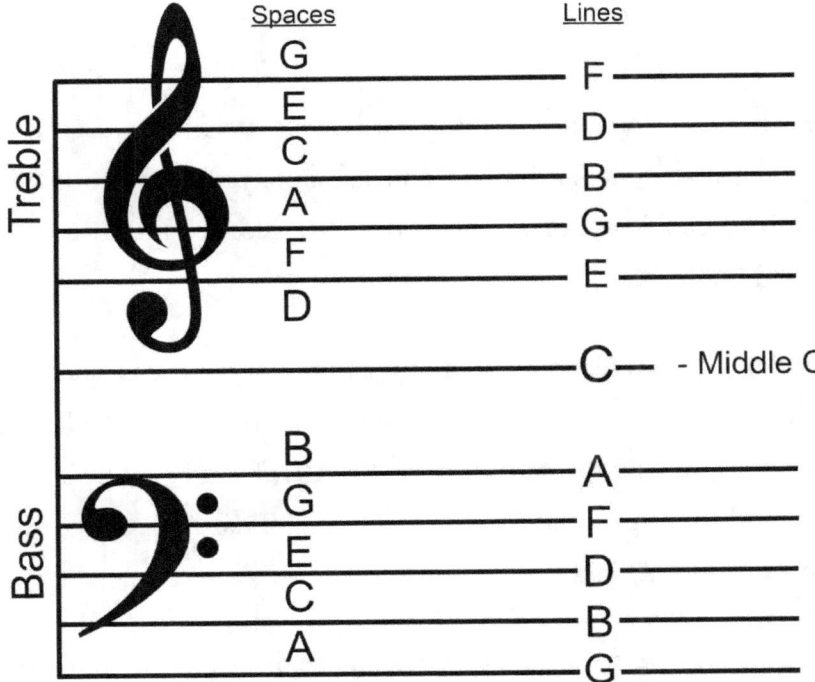

As you can see, there are five lines and four spaces on the staff. Notes can be written on each of these lines and spaces to create different melodies and songs.

When you're reading music, you'll need to use the staff to figure out which note to play on your instrument. So, the staff is a really important part of learning how to read music!

Treble Clef

Treble clef is a symbol used in sheet music to tell us how high or low a note is. When we see the treble clef, we know we are reading music meant to be played with the right hand on the piano.

The treble clef is made up of five lines and four spaces, and each line and space represents a different note. To remember which note is on each line, we can use a silly sentence like "Every Good Boy Deserves Fudge." Each word in the sentence starts with the first letter of the note name in order from bottom to top on the staff. So, the first line on the staff is E, the second line is G, the third line is B, the fourth line is D, and the fifth line is F.

To remember which note is on each space, we can use the word "FACE." The first space is F, the second space is A, the third space is C, and the fourth space is E.

So, when we read music in treble clef, we can look at the notes on the staff and know which note to play on the piano. With a little practice, we can read simple songs and play them on the piano!

Bass Clef

Just like the treble clef, the bass clef is also used to read music. It's mainly used for lower-pitched instruments like the bass guitar, cello, and tuba. On the piano, your left hand will be taking care of the bass notes. The bass clef looks different from the treble clef because it has two dots on either side of the second line.

To read music in bass clef, you can use some easy-to-remember phrases called mnemonics. The lines in the bass clef, from bottom to top, are remembered by the phrase: "Good Boys Do Fine Always." Each letter in that phrase represents a note: G, B, D, F, and A. The spaces between the lines are remembered by the phrase: "All Cows Eat Grass." That means that the notes on the spaces are A, C, E, and G (*Bass clef,* n.d.).

So when you see sheet music written in bass clef, you can use these phrases to help you remember the notes. With a little practice, you'll be able to read music in both treble and bass clef like a pro!

Symbols and Notes on the Staff

When you look at sheet music, you'll see different symbols that tell you how to play a song. The most critical symbols are the notes themselves, which tell you which sound to play. Notes are written on the staff, which is a set of five lines and four spaces.

In addition to notes, you'll also see other symbols on sheet music. Rests are symbols that tell you when to pause or stop playing. They look similar to notes, but they have different shapes and positions on the staff. For example, a quarter rest looks like a squiggly line and is placed on the middle line of the staff.

Other symbols you might see include sharps, flats, and naturals. These symbols change the pitch of a note. A sharp (#) raises a note by a half step, while a flat (b) lowers a note by a half step. A natural symbol cancels out a sharp or flat and returns the note to its original pitch (*Learn how to read sheet music: notes for music,* 2015).

Understanding these symbols and notes on the staff will help you read sheet music and play songs on your instrument!

Note Values

Note values are used to tell you how long to hold a note when playing music. We will learn about three main types of notes: quarter notes, half notes, and whole notes.

Counts	Note Value	Rest Value
Whole = 4 Counts	𝅝	▬
Half = 2 Counts	𝅗𝅥	▬
Quarter = 1 Count	𝅘𝅥	𝄽
Eighth = Half Count	𝅘𝅥𝅮	𝄾
Dotted Half Note = 3 Counts	𝅗𝅥.	

A quarter note looks like a filled-in circle with a straight stem. It represents one beat of sound. When you play a quarter note, you hold it for one count.

A half note looks like a circle with a straight stem that is open on the inside. It represents two beats of sound. When you play a half note, you hold it for two counts.

A whole note looks like a circle that is filled in and doesn't have a stem. It represents four beats of sound. When you play a whole note, you hold it for four counts.

There are also notes called dotted notes. A dot next to a note adds half of its value to the note (*How to count and play quarter notes on the piano,* n.d.). For example, a dotted half note would last for three counts (two beats for the half note and one beat for the dot).

An eighth note looks like a quarter note with a tail. This represents a one-half beat of sound. When you play an eighth note, you will play it for a half count.

Remember, these note values are like a recipe for playing music. By reading sheet music with different note values, you can play songs with different rhythms and beats.

Rests

When you play music, it's not just about the notes you play, but also about when you stop playing. That's where rests come in.

Rests are symbols in sheet music that show you when to take a break from playing. Just like notes, they have different shapes that tell you how long you should rest.

There are four main types of rests: whole rests, half rests, quarter rests, and eighth rests (*How to count and play quarter notes on the piano,* n.d.). The beat of each rest matches the beat of the note with the same name. So a whole rest looks like a box hanging from the fourth line, a half rest looks like a hat sitting on the third line, a quarter rest looks like a sideways "Z" sitting on the second line, and an eighth rest looks like a small flag sitting on the top line.

Just like with notes, rests also have different values that tell you how long you should rest for. A whole rest is equal to four beats, a half rest is equal to two beats, a quarter rest is equal to one beat, and an eighth rest is equal to half a beat.

So, when you see a rest in the sheet music, make sure to give yourself a little break and not play anything until the next note or rest comes along.

Tempo

Tempo is a fancy music word that means how fast or slow a song is played. It's like how fast or slow you walk or run.

When you look at sheet music, you will see some words that tell you how fast or slow to play the song. These words are called tempo markings.

For example, if you see the word "Allegro," you should play the song at a fast tempo. If you see the word "Adagio," you should play the song at a slow tempo.

So, tempo helps us understand how a song should be played, whether fast and exciting or slow and peaceful.

Simple Rhythms

When we play music, we need to follow a rhythm. That means playing notes for a certain amount of time and then taking breaks for a certain amount of time.

Steps and Skips

On the staff, steps and skips look like a series of notes that are either next to each other or have a space in between them on the keyboard. When notes are right next to each other on the keyboard, they are steps. While notes are separated by a note between them that is a skip. For example, C to E is a skip since D is in the middle. You can tell if a note is a step or a skip based on how close or far apart they are on the staff.

Slurs and Ties

On the staff, ties and slurs look like curved lines that connect two or more notes. Ties look like a curved line that connects two of the same notes, while slurs connect two or more different notes. When you see a tie or a slur in music, it means that the notes should be played smoothly and connected together, either by holding the same note for a longer time or by playing the notes smoothly without stopping in between.

Easy Rhythm Patterns

When we play music, we follow a pattern of notes and rests to create a rhythm. This rhythm is like a beat that helps us keep track of when to play each note. There are many different rhythms we can use to create music, but some are easier for beginners to learn.

One way to create rhythm on the piano is by using simple patterns. These patterns are made up of a few notes that we play over and over again. For example, we might play two quarter notes and a half note. This creates a pattern we can repeat throughout a song to give it a certain feeling.

There are many different rhythm patterns to choose from, and some are easier than others. Two common patterns for beginners are the "boom-chick" pattern and the "rockin' bass" pattern. The boom-chick pattern is made up of a quarter note followed by two eighth notes, and the rockin' bass pattern is made up of a quarter note followed by two half notes.

When we play a song, we usually start on the first beat of the first measure. But sometimes, the song might start with a few notes before the first beat. This is called a pick-up measure, and it helps us get a feel for the rhythm before we start playing the song for real.

By learning simple rhythm patterns, we can create music that sounds great and is easy to play. With practice, we can even start creating our own patterns and making music that is truly unique.

When you learn how to play a song, you might learn how to play it exactly the way the composer wrote it. But that doesn't mean you can't make it your own! Once you know the rules of how to play a song, you can start to add your own style and make it sound different from how anyone else plays it. A famous jazz musician named Duke Ellington did this by taking classical music songs and making them into jazz music. But before he could do that, he had to learn how to play the songs just like the composer wrote them.

ACTIVITY TIME: GUESS THE REST!

Let me tell you about a fun game called "Guess the Rest" that you can play with your parent/guardian/music teacher! It's all about learning the different types of rests in music.

First, your parent/guardian/music teacher will show you pictures of different rests and their nicknames, like "the bat" or "the mini-car." Then, they will cover up one of the columns and ask you to guess which picture is hiding underneath.

They'll give you clues to help you remember, like, "Which one looks like a lightning bolt?" or "Which one is worth two beats?" You'll have to use your memory and knowledge of rests to guess correctly!

This game is really fun and helps you remember all the different types of rests. Plus, once you know them all, you'll be able to spot them easily when you're reading music. Ask your parent/guardian/music teacher to play "Guess the Rest" with you and have fun learning about rests in music!

ACTIVITY TIME: CLAPPING SONGS!

Here are some fun games you can play with your music teacher or friends that will help you learn how to coordinate your clapping and singing!

A Sailor Went to Sea Sea Sea

"A Sailor Went to Sea Sea Sea" is a clapping game that involves a partner and a series of movements added with each verse. To start the game, sit facing your partner and clap your own hands together once. After that, you clap your partner's hands once, your left hand clapping their left hand. Then clap your own hands together, and then you and your partner clap your right hands together. Clap your own hands together once before either you clap your own hands three times or make a visor motion above your eyes three times. This is the basic clapping sequence for the game.

As you sing the song, you add a new movement with each verse that you do, along with the clapping (*Clap your hands: 16 clapping games for children's choir*, n.d.). Here are the lyrics and movements for each verse:

Verse 1: "A sailor went to sea sea sea, To see what he could see see see, But all that he could see see see, Was the bottom of the deep blue sea sea sea."

The clapping sequence will look like this: "A (clap own hands) sai– (clap left hands with partner together) –lor (clap own hands together) went (clap right hands with partners together) to (clap own hands together) sea sea sea (either clap your hands three times together or make three visor motions with your hands above your eyes)." This is the basic clapping and movement sequence for the game and the beat follows the syllables for the game. After some practice, you should get the hang of it pretty quick!

Verse 2: "A sailor went to chop chop chop, To see what he could chop chop chop, But all that he could chop chop chop, Was the bottom of the deep blue sea sea sea."

For this verse, you might chop your own hand or arm on "chop" and then do the regular clapping sequence.

Verse 3: "A sailor went to knee knee knee, To see what he could knee knee knee, But all that he could knee knee knee, Was the bottom of the deep blue sea sea sea."

For this verse, you might touch your knee on "knee" and then do the regular clapping sequence.

Verse 4: "A sailor went to door door door, To see what he could door door door, But all that he could door door door, Was the bottom of the deep blue sea sea sea."

For this verse, you might pretend to knock on a door on "door" and then do the regular clapping sequence.

The movements for each verse can vary, and you can get creative with them! Just remember to do the basic clapping sequence after each movement. The game is great for improving your coordination skills, as well as your ability to keep a steady beat. Have fun!

Quack Diddly Oso

"Quack Diddly Oso" is a fun clapping game that is similar to the popular game "Duck-Duck-Goose." In this game, you sit in a circle with a group of people.

To start the game, someone begins by making a simple clapping pattern, which is then passed around the circle. The clapping pattern goes around the circle until the person clapping decides to choose someone to be "it." When they choose someone, they say, "Quack Diddly Oso" and the person they choose becomes "it."

The person who is "it" then chases the person who passed the clap around the circle, trying to catch them before they reach their spot in the circle or across the room. If the person is caught, they become "it," and the game starts again.

You can keep playing until everyone has had a chance to be "it" or until you're ready to move on to a different game. This game is a great way to practice your clapping skills and coordination while also having fun with your friends!

WHAT DID WE LEARN?

Let's check out what we've learned in this chapter!

- Can you name a few different tempo markings?
- How does the tempo affect the mood of a piece of music?
- What is a tie?
- What is a slur?
- What are the different types of notes?

- Can you name a few notes and their durations?
- What is the treble clef?
- What kind of notes does the treble clef represent?
- What is the bass clef?
- What kind of notes does the bass clef represent?
- What is rhythm?
- What are beats?
- Can you clap out a simple rhythm pattern?
- What is the staff?
- How many lines and spaces are on the staff?

You're on a roll! You've finished another amazing chapter and learned all about the different notes, rhythms, and tempos you will discover as you learn the piano. And look, you've earned another gold star!

Great job! In this chapter, we've covered some fundamental music concepts, including the staff, rhythm, treble clef, bass clef, tempo, ties and slurs, and different note types. It's essential to understand these concepts before moving on to more advanced topics. Remember to practice these concepts as much as you can so that you can master them.

In the next chapter, we will focus on exercises and songs using one hand. These exercises will help you develop finger independence and strength in each hand, which are essential skills for playing any musical instrument. We will also explore some simple songs you can play with just one hand. By the end of this chapter, you'll be able to play some fun tunes while continuing to build your musical skills. So let's get started!

Hey there, fellow music enthusiasts!

Are you ready to unlock the musical magic of the piano and embark on a musical journey like no other? If you've already enjoyed the delightful book "Beginner Piano Lessons for Kids," we need your help to spread the joy and encourage others to join in on the harmonious fun! By leaving a review, you'll help aspiring pianists find the perfect guide and contribute to a world filled with more beautiful music. Here's a question: have you ever considered how helping others can make a difference?

Leaving a review for "Beginner Piano Lessons for Kids" is your chance to deliver value to others. By sharing your experience, insights, and thoughts, you can help potential readers or listeners understand the true worth of this fantastic book. Whether you found it to be an absolute game-changer in your child's musical journey or simply a delightful resource filled with engaging lessons, your review will guide others in their decision-making process.

Your review is crucial because countless parents and young learners are searching for the perfect piano book but are overwhelmed by the vast selection available. Your words can shine a light on the brilliance of "Beginner Piano Lessons for Kids" and give them the confidence to take the plunge. Imagine the smiles on their faces as they discover the joy of creating music and the gratitude they'll feel toward you for sharing your thoughts!

So, here's our humble request: please take a moment to leave an honest review for "Beginner Piano Lessons for Kids" on your favorite online platform. Whether it's Amazon, Goodreads, or any other website where you purchased or discovered the book, your feedback matters immensely. It's super easy to do! Head to the book's page, scroll down to the review section and let your fingers dance across the keyboard as you type your thoughts.

By leaving a review, you become part of a beautiful community of music lovers passionate about sharing their experiences. Your words can profoundly impact someone else's life, sparking a love for music that will last a lifetime. Isn't it amazing to think that a few minutes of your time can positively impact someone else's journey?

So, what are you waiting for? Grab your favorite device, hop onto your preferred online platform, and tell the world how "Beginner Piano Lessons for Kids" has enriched your musical experience. Remember, your review can ignite a passion for piano in others and bring a symphony of joy to countless lives.

Thank you from the bottom of our musical hearts!

CHAPTER 5:

Piano Mastery Pt. 1—One-Handed Wonders

Beginner Piano Lessons for Kids

Taylor Kent W.

Cool Fact #5: Jimmy Liu, a boy from Tennessee, can play the piano with one hand and solve a Rubik's cube with the other!

How does Jimmy do it? Well, it's all about practice, my friend. Jimmy spends hours and hours honing his piano skills and challenging himself with the Rubik's cube. He's got the fingers of a pianist and the mind of a puzzle genius. He's figured out the secret moves to create stunning melodies and solve the Rubik's cube like a pro.

Jimmy's talent reminds us that with dedication and practice, we can achieve incredible things. So, the next time you feel inspired, grab a musical instrument or a puzzle and let your own unique talents shine. Who knows, maybe you'll be the next superstar who can play the piano with one hand and conquer a puzzle with the other!

So, go out there and explore the wonders of music and puzzles, and who knows what amazing things you'll discover!

In this chapter, we will be exploring ways to improve your piano-playing skills with exercises designed to help you focus on using only one hand. Whether you're a beginner or an advanced pianist, learning to play with one hand can be challenging, but with practice and dedication, it can also be incredibly rewarding. In this chapter, we will introduce you to a variety of exercises and songs that are specifically designed to help you improve your playing with one hand. We'll explore the benefits of playing with one hand, provide tips for mastering this technique, and give you plenty of opportunities to practice your skills. So, let's dive in and explore the world of piano playing with one hand!

MAJOR SCALES FOR RIGHT-HAND PRACTICE

In Chapter 3, we learned about finger exercises to help build strength and dexterity in both hands. Now, we will focus on practicing with the right hand, specifically by learning major scales. Scales are an important aspect of playing piano, as they help to develop finger coordination and technique. In this section, we will explore the major scales and provide exercises to help you practice them with your right hand. By practicing these scales regularly, you'll not only improve your right-hand technique but also develop your understanding of music theory and how different notes and chords relate to each other. So, let's get started with practicing major scales for right-hand practice!

What Is a Scale?

A scale is like a special group of notes that sounds good together in a song. It has a key note that starts the group, and every other note in the scale is related to that key note. If a song uses notes from the C major scale, it means that the song is in the key of C major (*All major and minor scales [including fingering for piano]*, 2020).

Major Scales

Major scales are very important to learn when playing piano because they are used a lot in happy and cheerful music. They are usually the first scales people learn on the piano because they are so common. A lot of songs that you might hear on the radio use major scales. This means to play some of your favorite songs, you might need to use these scales!

C Major Scale

Let's start practicing the C major scale! It's a really fun and easy scale to learn. When you play the C major scale, you only need to use the white keys on the piano.

First, you'll want to practice playing the scale with one hand at a time. Use the fingering numbers under each note to help guide you. Practice slowly and carefully, making sure your fingers hit the right keys.

Once you feel comfortable playing with one hand, it's time to practice both hands together. This can be a bit tricky at first, but keep practicing! Start at a slow tempo using a metronome to keep you on beat, and gradually speed up as you get better.

Remember to take breaks when you need to and have fun while practicing the C major scale. It's an essential skill to learn as it's used in a lot of different types of music.

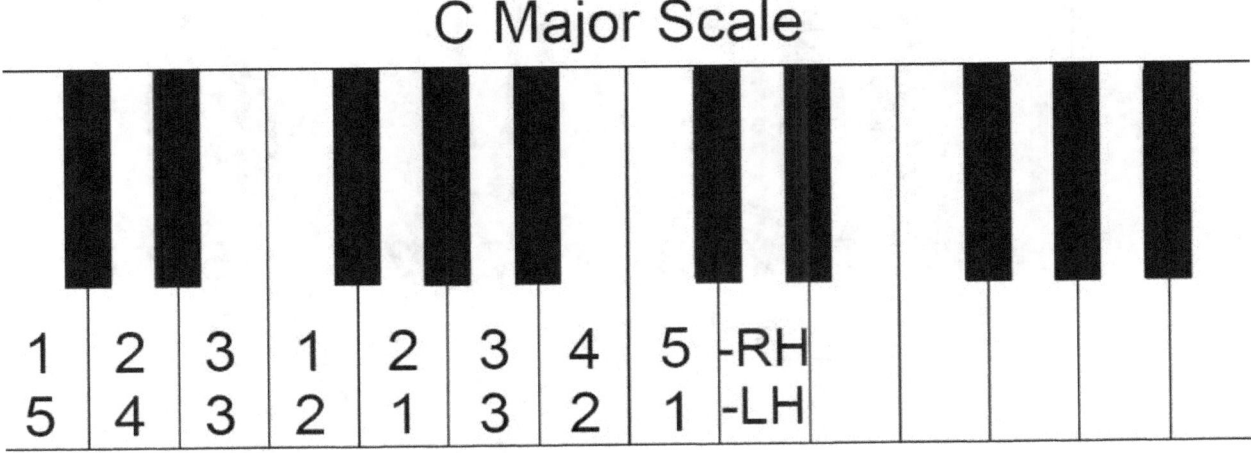

Here are three popular songs in the key of C major:

- "Happy" by Pharrell Williams
- "Let It Be" by The Beatles
- "Can't Stop the Feeling" by Justin Timberlake

G Major Scale

Now it's time to learn a new scale! The G major scale is the next one I want to teach you. It's called G major because it starts on the note G. Remember how C major had no sharps? Well, G major has just one sharp note to remember—it's called F# and it's the only black key you'll need to use for this scale.

To play the G major scale on the piano, you'll need to use the white keys except for that one black key we just talked about. You'll use the same fingers as you did for the C major scale, so it's not too hard to learn.

This is a two-octave scale, which means you'll be playing a lot of notes. But don't worry, just take it one note at a time and soon you'll be playing the whole thing with ease!

G Major Scale

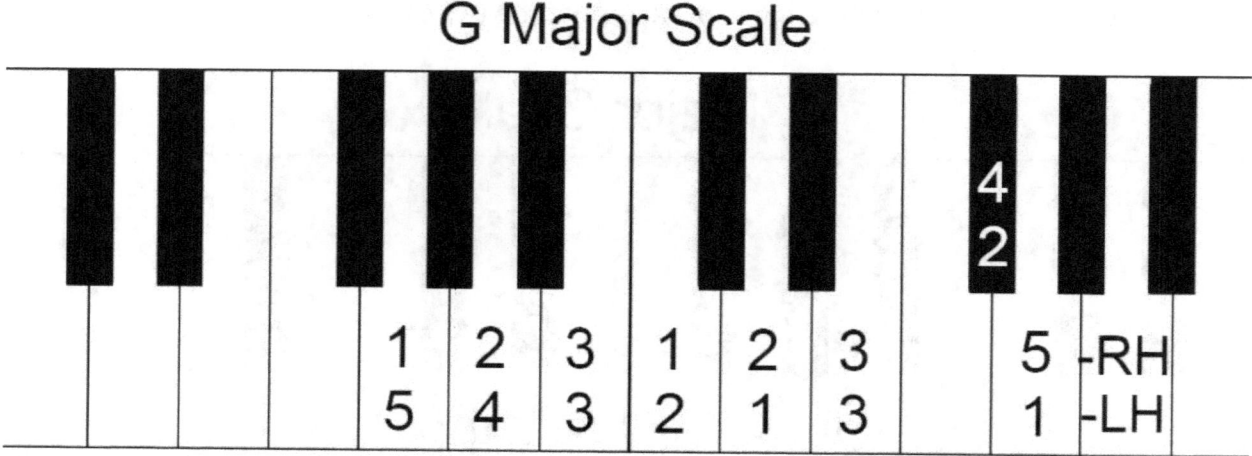

Here are three popular songs in the key of G major:

- "Sweet Home Alabama" by Lynyrd Skynyrd
- "Love Story" by Taylor Swift
- "Free Fallin" by Tom Petty

D Major Scale

Are you ready to learn another scale? This time it's the D major scale! This scale is a little trickier than the previous scales we've learned, but you can do it!

The D major scale includes the notes D, E, F#, G, A, B, and C#. You'll notice that there are two sharps in this scale, which means you'll be playing two black keys on the piano. But don't worry; it's not that hard!

To play the D major scale with your right hand, start with your thumb on the D note and cross your thumb under to play the G note. With your left hand, cross your middle finger over to play the B note.

Here's the D major scale with the fingering numbers under each note. Practice one hand at a time and then both hands together to make it sound smooth and easy.

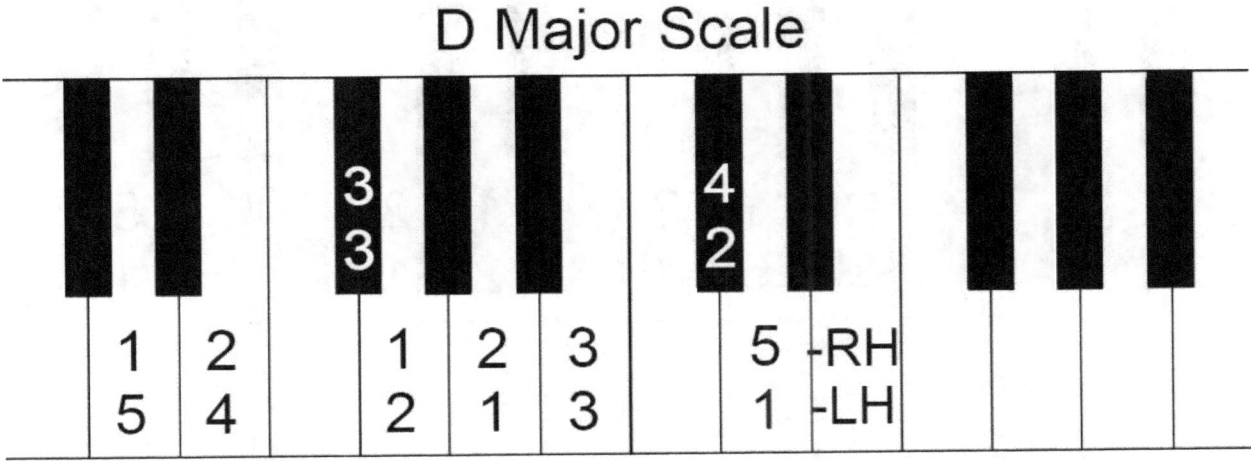

Here are three popular songs in D major:

- "Thinking Out Loud" by Ed Sheeran
- "Pompeii" by Bastille
- "Viva la Vida" by Coldplay

A Major Scale

Alright, now we're up to the A major scale. This one has a bit more of a challenge than the previous scales, as it has three sharps. The A major scale goes like this: A, B, C#, D, E, F#, G#, and A. This means you'll have to play on three black keys: C#, F#, and G#. Don't worry, though! If you have been practicing the previous scales, you will be ready for this one.

The finger pattern for A major is the same as the other scales, so you don't have to learn anything new. Just follow the written instructions under each note to know which finger to use.

Here is the scale of A major, with the corresponding fingerings under each note. Remember to practice with each hand separately first, then together.

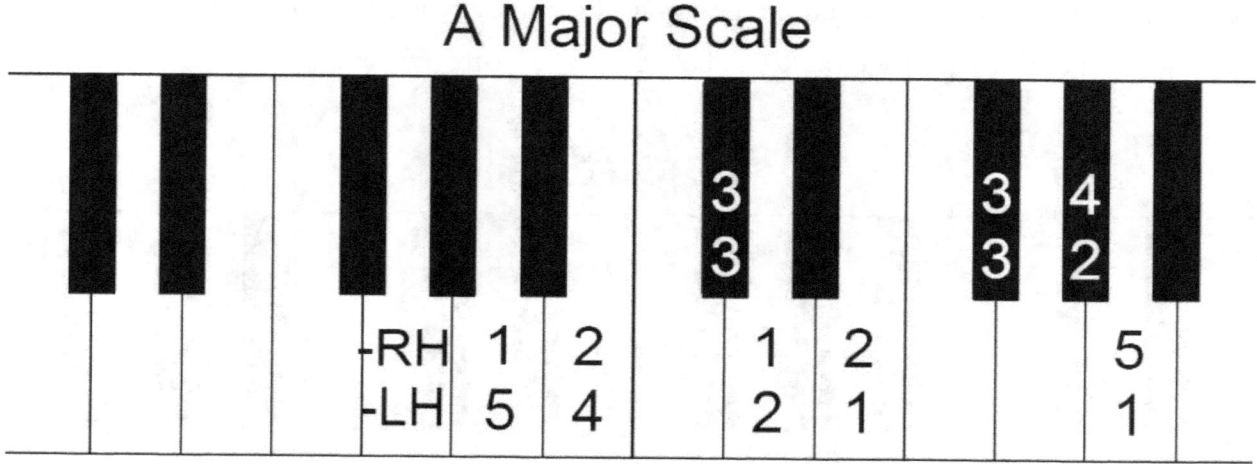

Here are three popular songs in A major:

- "Clocks" by Coldplay
- "Livin' on a Prayer" by Bon Jovi
- "Just the Way You Are" by Bruno Mars

E Major Scale

Now, we will introduce you to the E major scale, which has four sharps. The notes of this scale are E, F#, G#, A, B, C#, D#, and E. This means that you will be playing a lot of black keys! But don't worry, with practice, your fingers will get used to it.

To play this scale, use the same finger pattern as the other major scales. Remember to cross your thumb after the third finger on your right hand. When playing with your left hand, cross the middle finger over the thumb.

Below, you can see the written music of the E major scale. The numbers under each note tell you which finger to use. Keep practicing and don't forget the four sharps!

E Major Scale

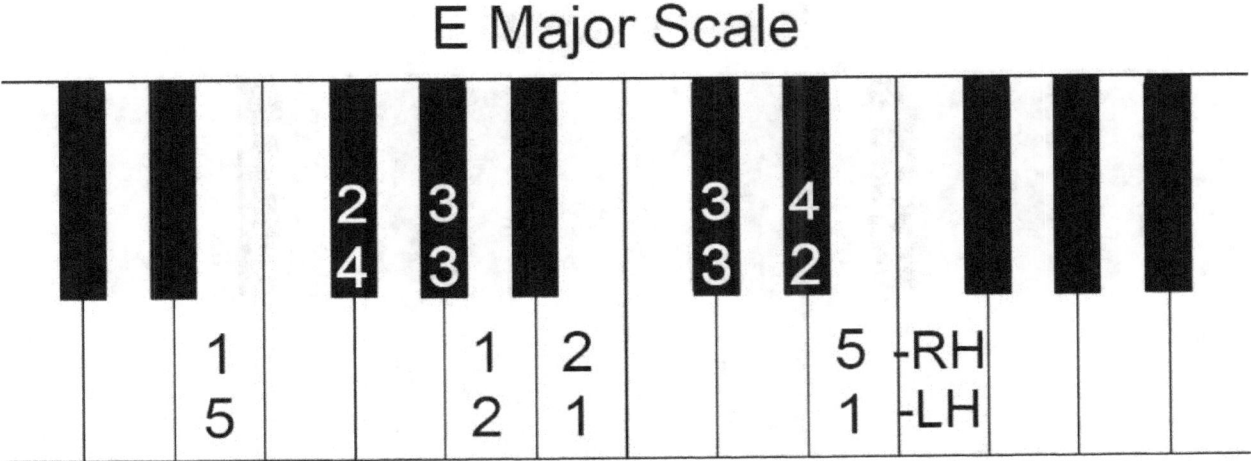

Here are three popular songs in E major:

- "Sweet Child o' Mine" by Guns N' Roses
- "Tears in Heaven" by Eric Clapton
- "Layla" by Eric Clapton

B Major Scale

Are you ready for the big challenge? The B major scale contains *five* sharps! That's a lot of black keys, so be ready to use your fingers and stretch them out.

To play the B major scale, you'll start with your right thumb on the B note and use your third finger to play the D# note. With your left hand, you'll cross your ring finger over your thumb to play the F# note.

Here is the guide for the B major scale, with the suggested fingering for each note. Take your time and practice each hand separately before attempting to play with both hands together. Good luck!

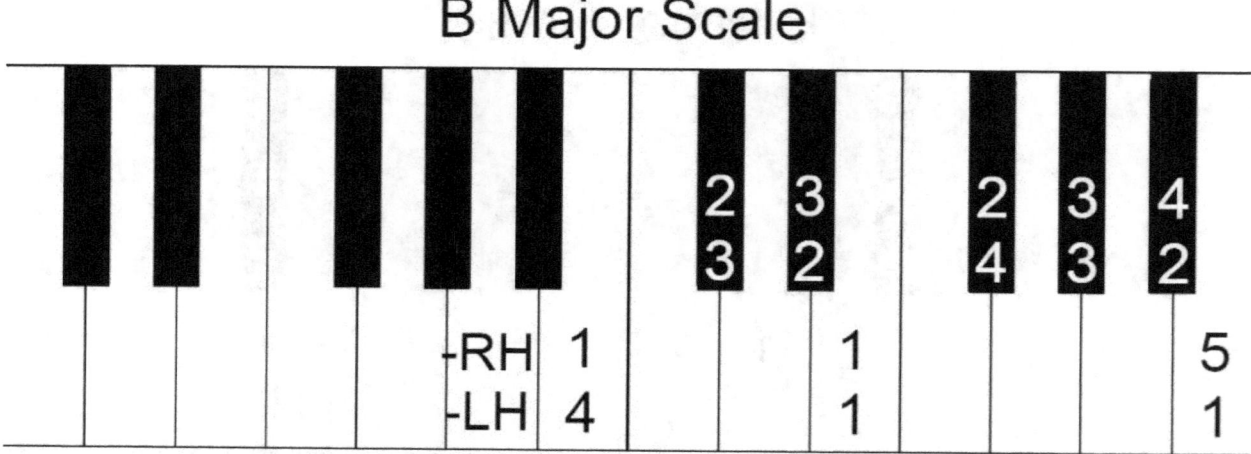

Here are three popular songs in B major:

- "Born In The USA" by Bruce Springsteen
- "Let It Be" by The Beatles
- "Halo" by Beyoncé

F Major Scale

Have you ever met someone who stands out from the others? Well, the F major scale is just like that person! This scale has a special note called a flat (B flat) instead of a sharp. The notes in the F major scale are F, G, A, B flat, C, D, E, and F.

To play the F major scale, you need to use a different finger pattern. Instead of switching to your thumb after the third note, switch after the *fourth* note on your right hand. This means you'll play the C note with your thumb.

Here's the F major scale with the recommended fingerings for each note. Have fun playing it!

F Major Scale

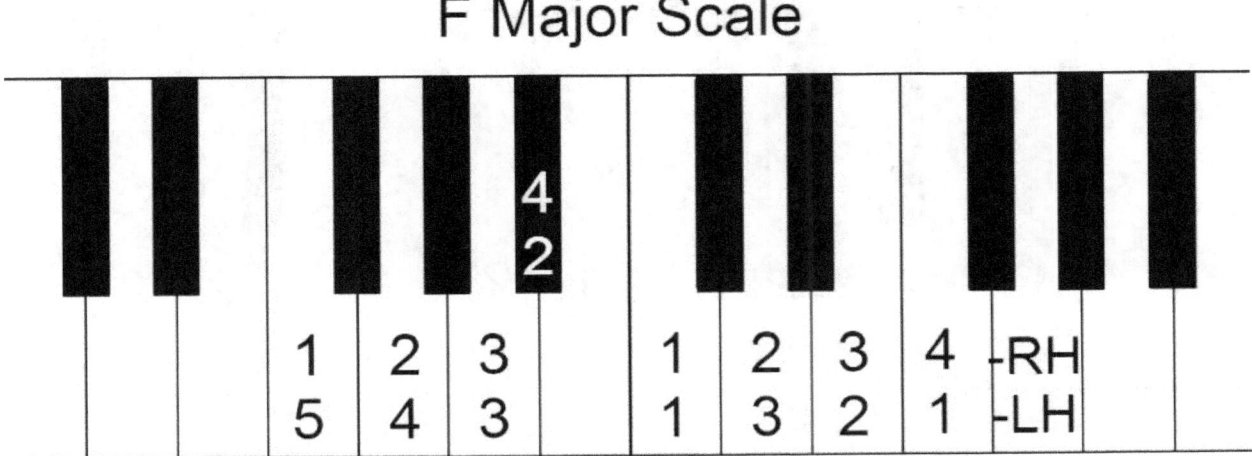

Here are three popular songs in F major:

- "Ain't No Sunshine" by Bill Withers
- "Say You Won't Let Go" by James Arthur
- "Someone Like You" by Adele

Bb/A# Major Scale

The Bb (or A#) major scale contains three flat/sharp notes. The notes in this scale are Bb (or A#), C, D, Eb (or D#), F, G, A, and Bb (or A#). To play this scale on the piano, you'll need to use your fingers in a particular order. Start with your right ring finger on Bb and work your way up the keyboard. Use your right middle finger to play the Eb note. When you reach the end of the scale, use your right ring finger to play the next Bb note. For the pattern with the left hand, start with your left middle finger on the lower Bb. Remember to use the correct finger for each note, and practice until you can play the scale smoothly and evenly!

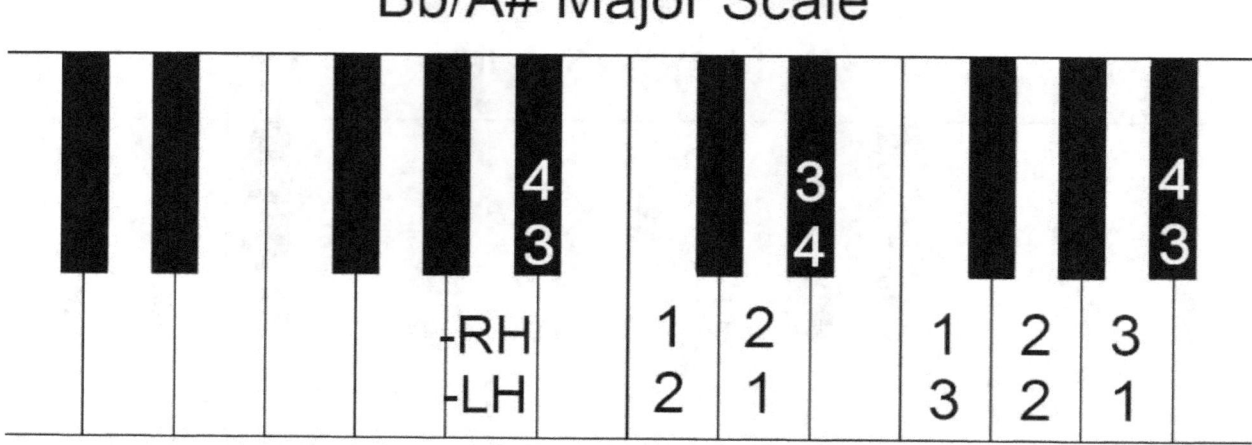

Here are three popular songs in the key of Bb/A# major:

- "Rolling in the Deep" by Adele
- "All About That Bass" by Meghan Trainor
- "Roar" by Katy Perry

Eb/D# Major Scale

The Eb/D# major scale is a fun one to play because it has three flats or sharps, depending on how you look at it! The notes in this scale are Eb, F, G, Ab, Bb, C, D, and Eb. To play this scale on the piano, start with your right middle finger on the Eb note, and cross your thumb under to play the F note. Keep going up and down the scale until you get to the high Eb note. Make sure to use the recommended fingerings for each note to help you play the scale smoothly. Have fun playing the Eb/D# major scale on the piano!

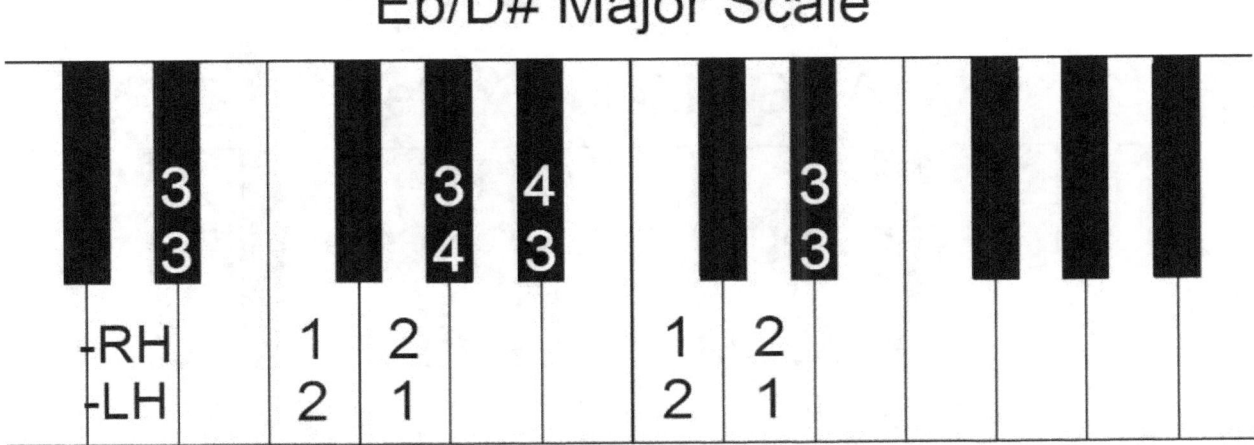

Here are three popular songs in the Eb/D# major scale:

- "My Heart Will Go On" by Celine Dion
- "All I Want for Christmas Is You" by Mariah Carey
- "Shape of You" by Ed Sheeran

Ab/G# Major Scale

Let's talk about the Ab/G# major scale! This scale has eight notes and it includes the notes Ab (which is the same as G#), Bb, C, Db (or C#), Eb (or D#), F, and G. It has *four* flats (or sharps, if you prefer to call them that).

The fingering for the right hand is similar to the other scales we have covered before. The left-hand fingering requires a bit of hand gymnastics. You start with your left middle finger and cross your left ring finger over your thumb to hit the Db/C#. Below is a picture of the Ab/G# major scale with the fingerings for each note. Give it a try and have fun!

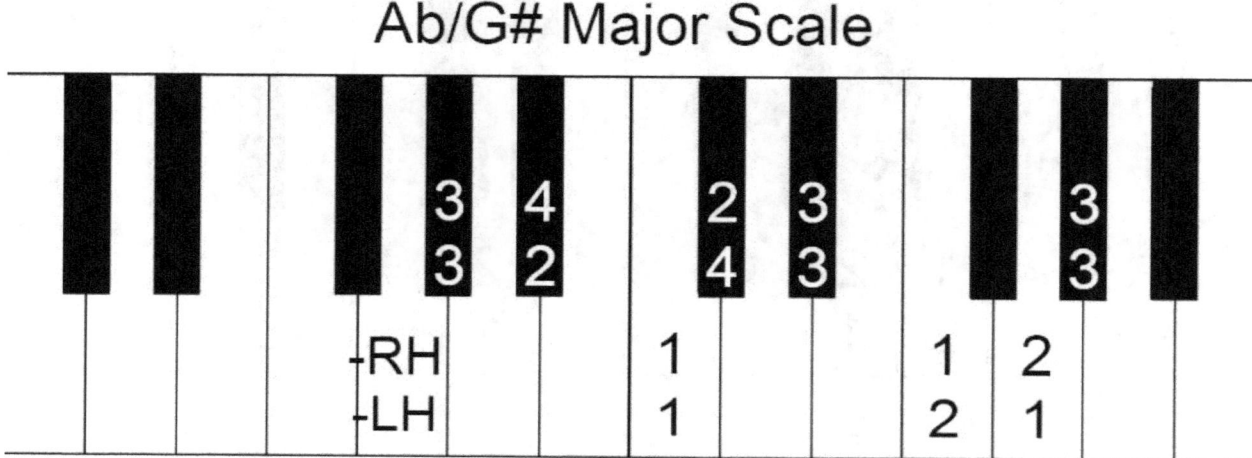

Here are three well-known songs in the Ab/G# Major Scale:

- "I Will Always Love You" by Whitney Houston
- "Clarity" by Zedd
- "Stay" by Rihanna ft. Mikky Ekko

Db/C# Major Scale

The Db/C# major scale consists of seven different notes: Db, Eb, F, Gb, Ab, Bb, and C. It might sound complicated, but once you get the hang of it, it's not too hard to play. To play this scale on the right hand, start with your right pointer finger on Db and follow the fingering pattern. For the left hand, start with your left middle finger on Db. Follow the fingering numbers for each and use your thumb to cross under after the third finger on your right hand.

Below is the Db/C# major scale written out with the suggested fingerings to use. Have fun playing!

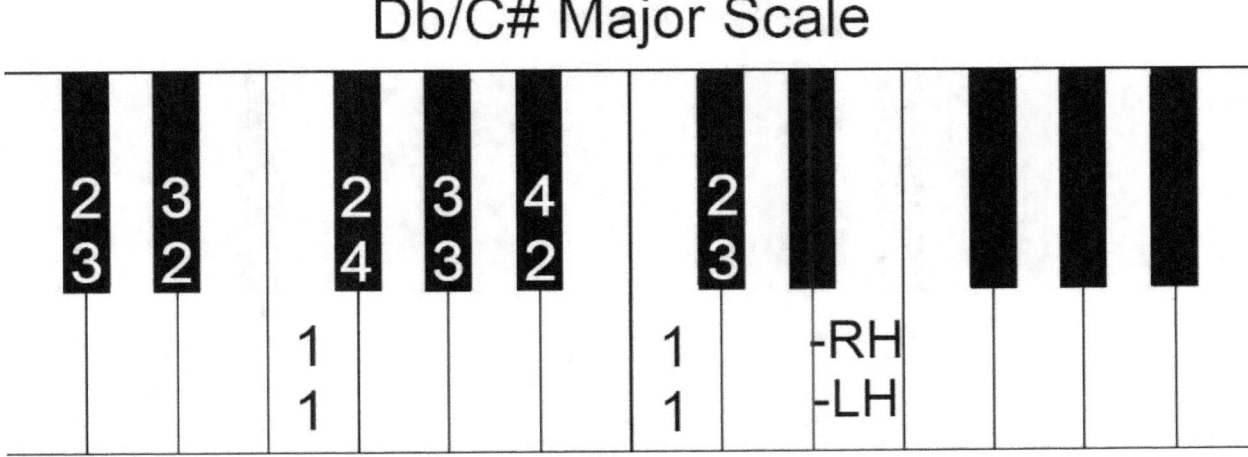

Here are three popular songs in the key of Db/C# major:

- "Unbreak My Heart" by Toni Braxton
- "No One" by Alicia Keys
- "I See Fire" by Ed Sheeran

F#/Gb Major Scale

The F# or Gb major scale is a little bit tricky because it has six sharps or flats in its key signature. The notes of the scale are F#, G#, A#, B, C#, D#, and F. To play this scale on the right hand, start with your right pointer finger on F# and continue the fingering pattern outlined in the diagram. Your right ring finger will play A# and your thumb will cross under to play B. Your right index will play C# and the finger pattern continues. When you reach your middle finger on D#, cross your thumb under to play F. Finally, use your right pointer finger to play the highest note, which is F#. Remember to use the suggested finger pattern for your left hand!

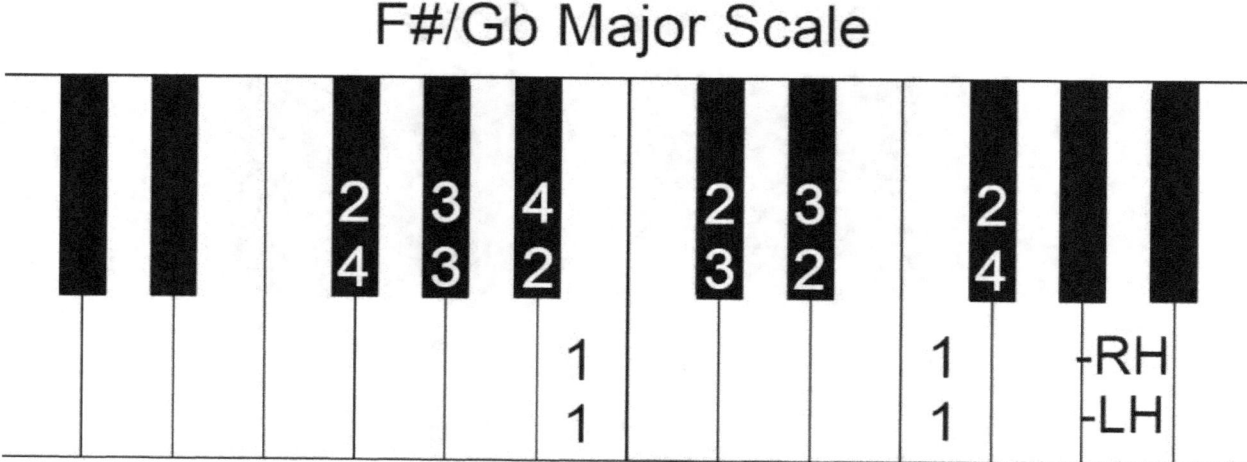

Here are three popular songs in the F#/Gb major scale:

- "You Belong With Me" by Taylor Swift
- "How You Remind Me" by Nickelback
- "Born This Way" by Lady Gaga

Exercises Using Major Scales

Here are three fun and easy exercises for young beginner piano players using the major scales and their right hand:

1. **Scale hopping:** Starting with the C major scale, play each note in a hopping motion. Begin with your thumb on C, then hop to your index finger on D, middle finger on E, and so on, until you reach your pinky on C. Once you've mastered the C major scale, move on to the other scales.

2. **Scale runs:** Start with your thumb on the first note of the C major scale and play each note in quick succession, moving up and down the scale with ease. Once you've practiced this exercise in C major, try it with the other scales.

3. **Scale patterns:** Using the C major scale, play the first three notes (C, D, E) with your thumb, index, and middle fingers. Press the fourth note (F) with your thumb and play the fifth note (G) with your index. Finally, play the sixth and seventh notes (A, B) with your middle finger and ring finger. Repeat this pattern up and down the scale.

This section has been all about playing happy-sounding music on the piano. We used something called major scales, which are like a group of special notes that we play in a special order. Major scales will always follow this formula—whole, whole, half, whole, whole, whole, half (*All major and minor scales [including fingering for piano]*, 2020). When we say whole or half, we are referring to the space between the keys. A whole step will always cross over a key, whereas a half step will always entail hitting the next key. This does not exclude the black keys! The order goes up and down and the last note is the same as the first note. Each scale has a different pattern and some of them have black keys called sharps or flats. We have learned about 12 different major scales and the songs we can play using them.

MINOR SCALES FOR RIGHT-HAND PRACTICE

In addition to major scales, there are also minor scales that can be played on the piano. Minor scales have a slightly different sequence of notes than major scales, and they often sound a little bit sadder or more mysterious. The pattern of whole and half steps in a minor scale is different than a major scale, and though they can share the same notes and keys, they are technically in a different key signature. Since the C major scale and A minor scale share the same notes, they will sound good together. The A minor scale is the relative minor to the C major scale. Feel free to play around with this in your free time when you find the patterns and similarities of these major and minor scales, though that isn't the focus here. A whole step is C to D, but a half step is C to C#. Though it will be a bit different from the major scale formula, the minor scale formula looks like this—whole, half, whole, whole, half, whole, whole. In this section, you will learn about the different types of minor scales, how to play them with your right hand, and some fun songs you can practice with each one (*All major and minor scales [including fingering for piano]*, 2020).

What Is a Minor Scale?

A minor scale is another musical scale used in music. It sounds a bit sad or moody compared to major scales, which usually sound happier. The pattern of notes in a minor scale is different from a major scale and has a different key signature. Like major scales, there are different types of minor scales (*All major and minor scales [including fingering for piano]*, 2020).

A Minor Scale

To play the A minor scale, place your right-hand thumb (finger 1) on the A note to start. Then, put your second finger on the next note up, which is B. After that, use your third finger to play the next note, C. Then, tuck your thumb under to the next note, D. Next, use your fingers in sequence to play the remaining notes. Practice playing the scale up and down with your right hand until you can play it smoothly and confidently.

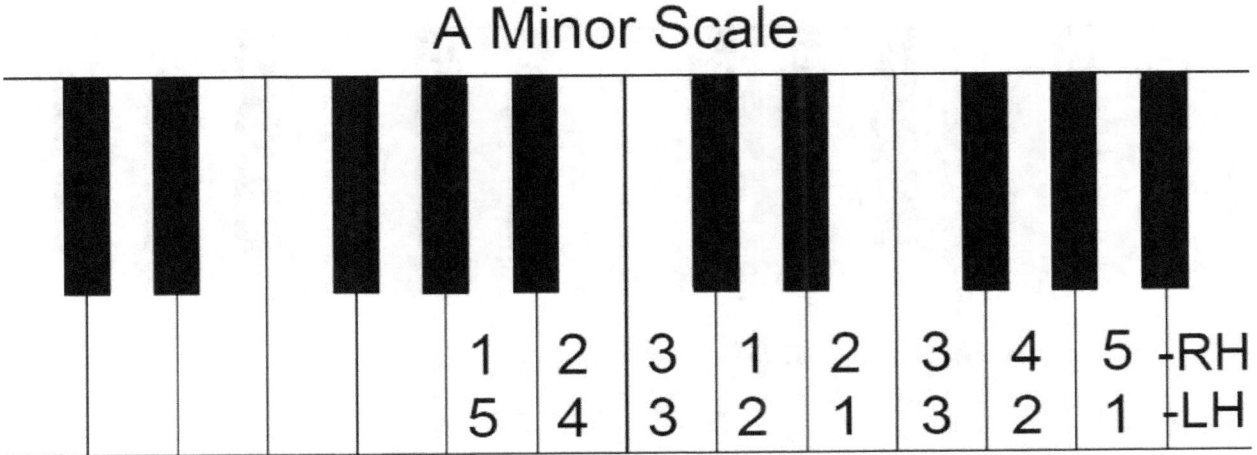

Here are three well-known songs in the A minor scale:

- "Stairway to Heaven" by Led Zeppelin
- "Don't Stop Believing" by Journey
- "All of Me" by John Legend

Bb/A# Minor Scale

To play the Bb/A# minor scale on the piano, you will need to place your right-hand fingers on the following keys in order: Bb, C, Db, Eb, F, Gb, Ab, Bb using the suggested fingering below. You can also play this scale with your left hand by starting on the lower Bb and going up to the higher Bb. With practice, you'll be able to play this scale smoothly and confidently!

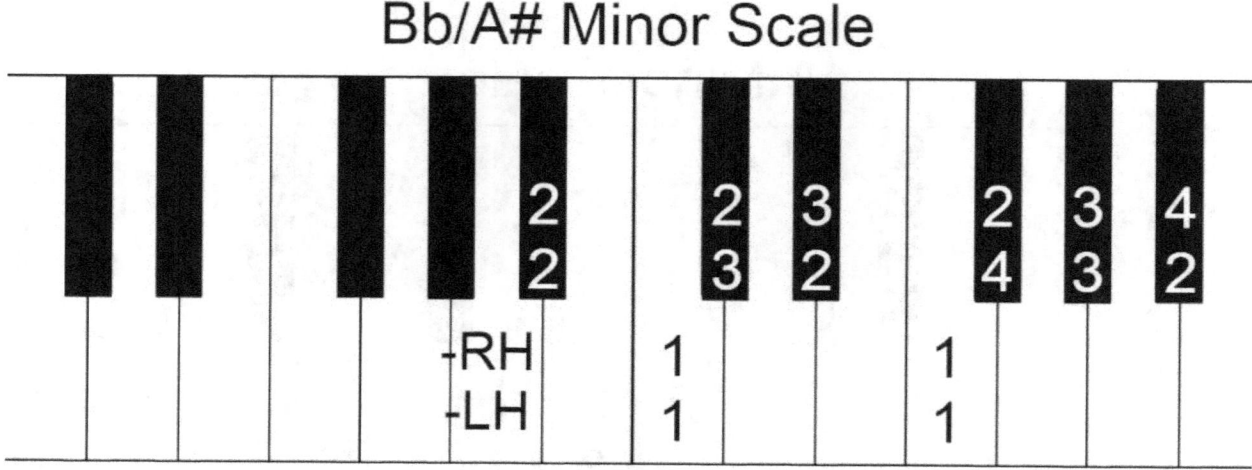

Here are some songs that contain sections that use notes from this scale:

- "All I Want" by Kodaline—The chorus of this song uses notes from the Bb/A# Minor Scale.
- "Someone You Loved" by Lewis Capaldi—The pre-chorus and chorus of this song use notes from the Bb/A# Minor Scale.
- "Heathens" by Twenty One Pilot—The verse and chorus of this song use notes from the Bb/A# Minor Scale.

B Minor Scale

To play the B minor scale on the piano, place your right-hand thumb on the B note just to the right of the group of 3 black keys. Place your second finger on the C# key, your third finger on the D note, and your thumb tucks under to play the E key. Then, your pointer finger plays F# and your fingers sequentially play the remaining notes of G, A, and B. Play the notes in order, from the lowest to the highest, and then back down.

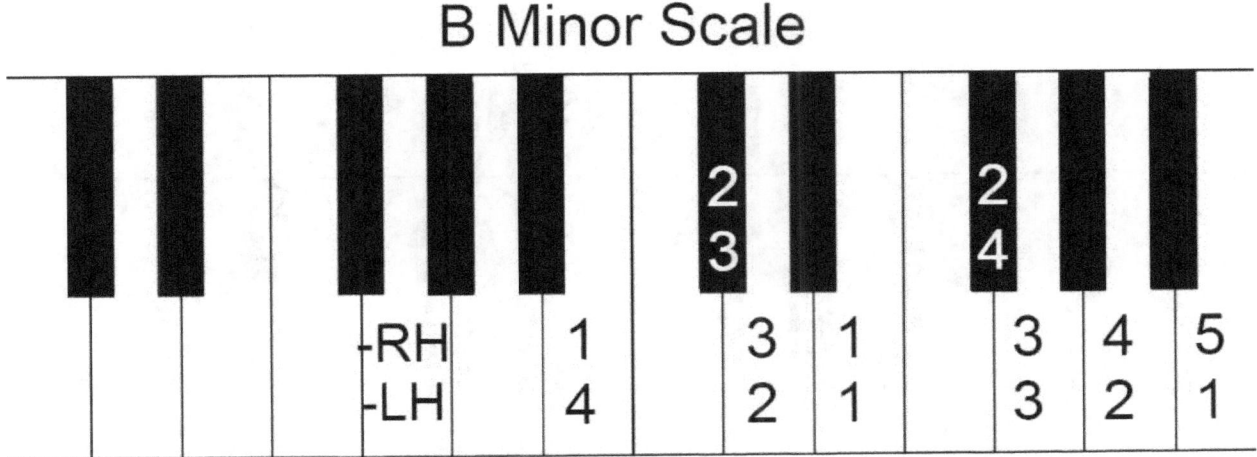

Here are three popular songs in the B minor scale:

- "Nothing Else Matters" by Metallica
- "All Along the Watchtower" by Jimi Hendrix
- "Iris" by The Goo Goo Dolls

C Minor Scale

To play the C minor scale on the piano, place your right-hand thumb on middle C. From there, place your second finger on the next white key to the right, which is D. Then, place your third finger on the next black key to the right, which is D#. After crossing your thumb under to play F, you will continue placing your fingers on the next white and black keys in sequence until you reach Bb with your ring finger and the next C with your pinky. Then, reverse the pattern by playing the same sequence of keys in reverse order, ending with your thumb back on middle C. Remember to keep your fingers curved and to press down on the keys firmly but not too hard.

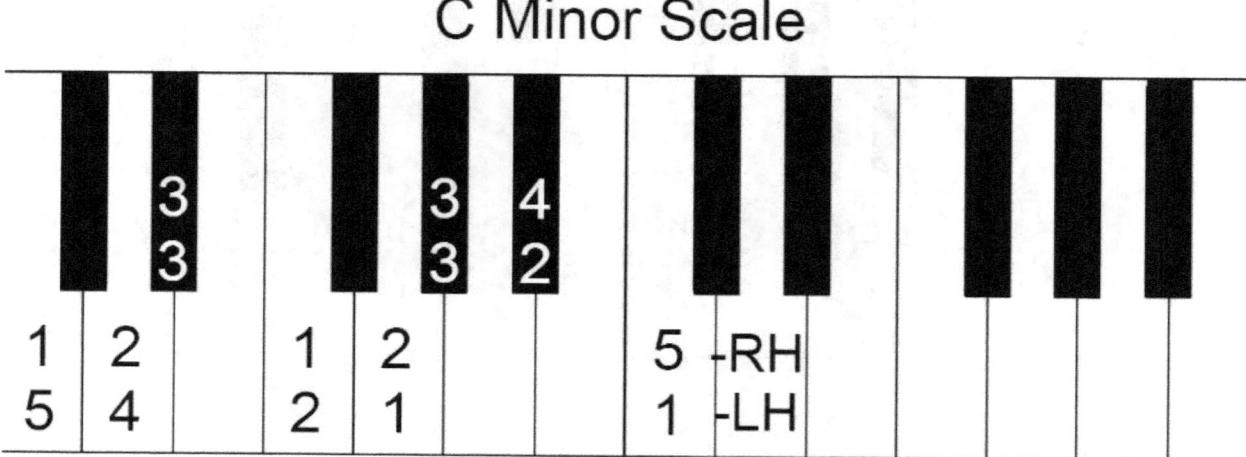

Three popular songs in C minor scale are:

- "Für Elise" by Ludwig van Beethoven
- "Toccata and Fugue in D Minor" by Johann Sebastian Bach (although it has some parts in C minor as well)
- "Moonlight Sonata" by Ludwig van Beethoven

C#/Db Minor Scale

To play the C#/Db minor scale on the piano, place your right middle finger (or left middle finger) on C#, which is the left back key in the pair of the group of two black keys. Then follow the pattern… continue until you reach the next C# or Db key with the middle finger of either hand. Remember to use the correct fingers for each key, and try to play each note evenly and smoothly.

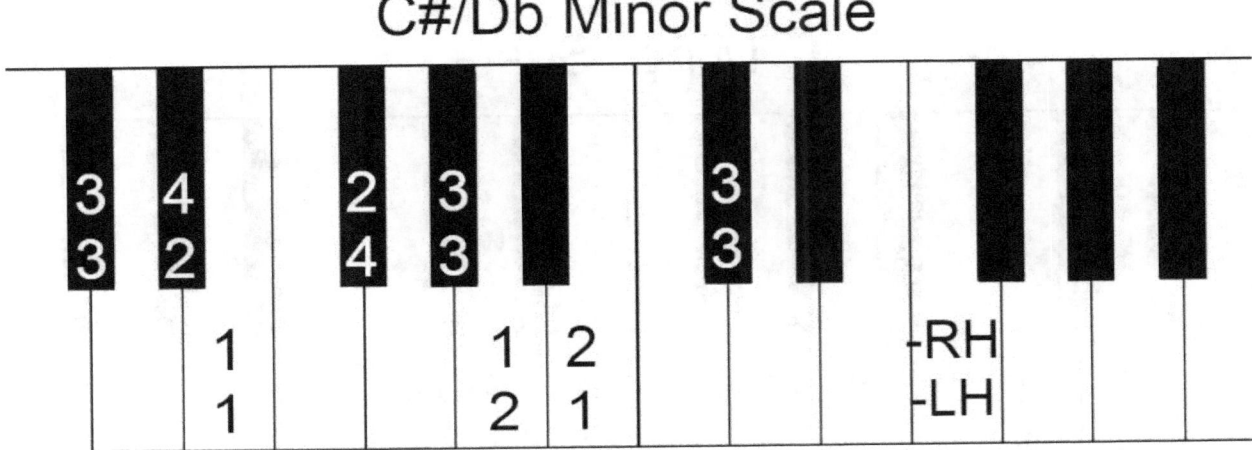

Here are three well-known songs in the C#/Db minor scale:

- "Nocturne in C-sharp minor" by Frédéric Chopin
- "One" by Metallica
- "Bittersweet Symphony" by The Verve

D Minor Scale

To play the D minor scale on the piano with your right hand, start by placing your thumb on the D note. Then, place your second finger on the E note, your third finger on the F note, your thumb crosses under to hit the G note, your pointer finger plays the A note, and your middle finger plays the Bb note, and finally, your right ring finger plays the C key then your pinky plays the last D key. Practice playing the notes up and down in a smooth and even motion, and pay attention to the correct finger placement for each note.

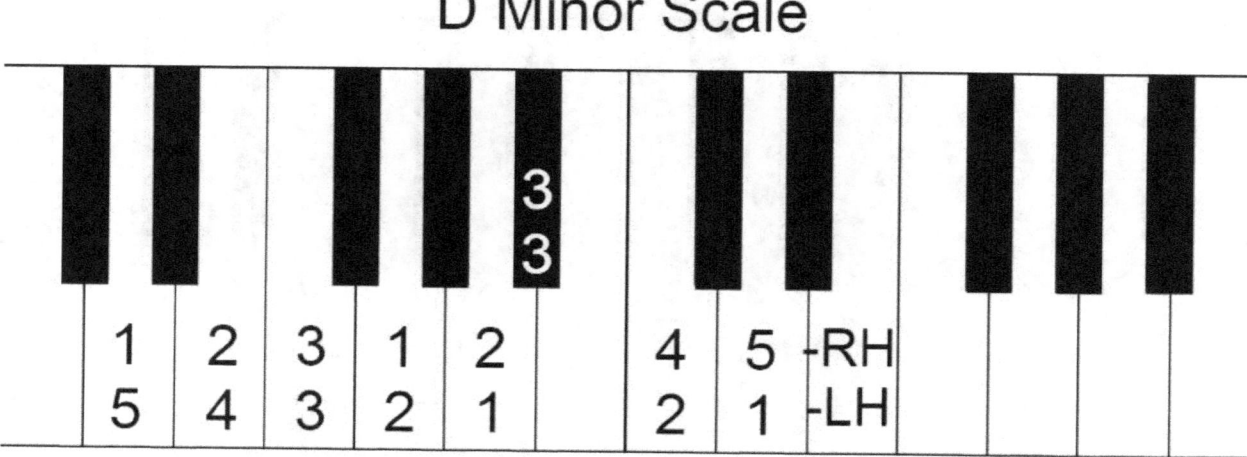

Here are three popular songs in the D minor scale:

- "Symphony No. 40" by Wolfgang Amadeus Mozart
- "Human" by Christina Perri
- "Sound of Silence" by Simon & Garfunkel

Eb/D# Minor Scale

To play the Eb/D# minor scale on the piano, place your right middle finger on the black key that is the right one of the group of two. This is the note Eb or D#. Then, follow the pattern of playing the keys in the sequence of whole, half, whole, whole, half, whole, and whole steps. The notes of this scale are: Eb, F, Gb, Ab, Bb, B, and Db. You can play the scale with the fingers on the right hand 3, 1, 2, 3, 4, 1, 2, and 3, respectively. To play the scale with the left hand, use the index finger, finger 2, to start playing the note Eb.

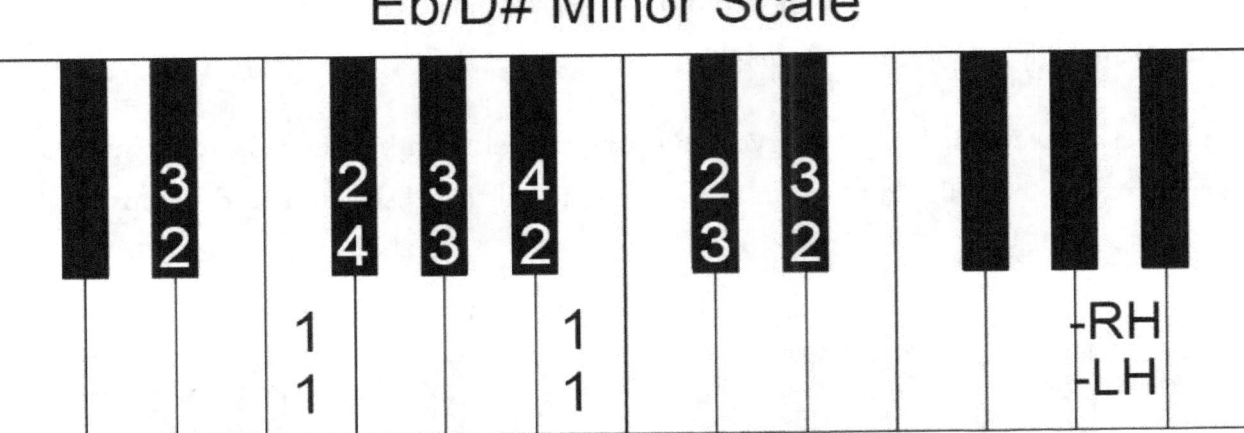

Here are three popular songs in the Eb/D# minor scale:

- "Human Nature" by Michael Jackson
- "When We Were Young" by Adele
- "In the End" by Linkin Park

E Minor Scale

E minor scale consists of seven notes, which are E, F#, G, A, B, C, and D. To play the E minor scale on the piano, place your right-hand thumb on the E note, which is the white key to the left of two black keys. Then, place your second finger on the F# note—the black key on the left of the group of three black keys. Then, place your third finger on the G note—the white key to the right of the F# key. Next, tuck your thumb under to reach the A note— the white key to the left of the rightmost black key. Next, use your pointer finger on the B note—the white key to the right of the group of 3 black keys. Finally, place your middle finger on the C note—the white key to the left of the group of two black keys. Then play the D note with your ring finger. Finally, play the E note with your pinky!

Remember to keep your fingers curved and play each note with the tip of your finger. Also, practice playing the scale slowly at first and then gradually increase your speed. Happy playing!

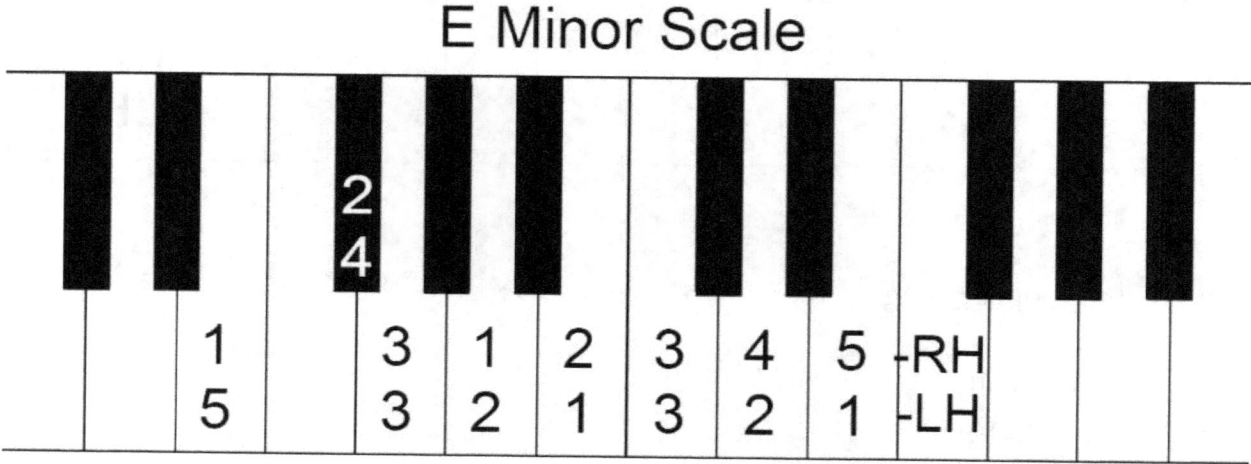

Here are three popular songs in the key of E minor:

- "Another One Bites The Dust" by Queen
- "Hallelujah" by Leonard Cohen
- "Boulevard of Broken Dreams" by Green Day

F Minor Scale

To play the F minor scale on the piano, start with your right-hand thumb on the F note, which is located just to the left of the set of three black keys. Play the following order with the fingers indicated: 1 (thumb), 2, 3, 4, 1, 2, 3, and 4. This will take you up to the higher F note. To come back down the scale, play the same notes in reverse order. Make sure to use the correct finger for each note to develop the proper technique.

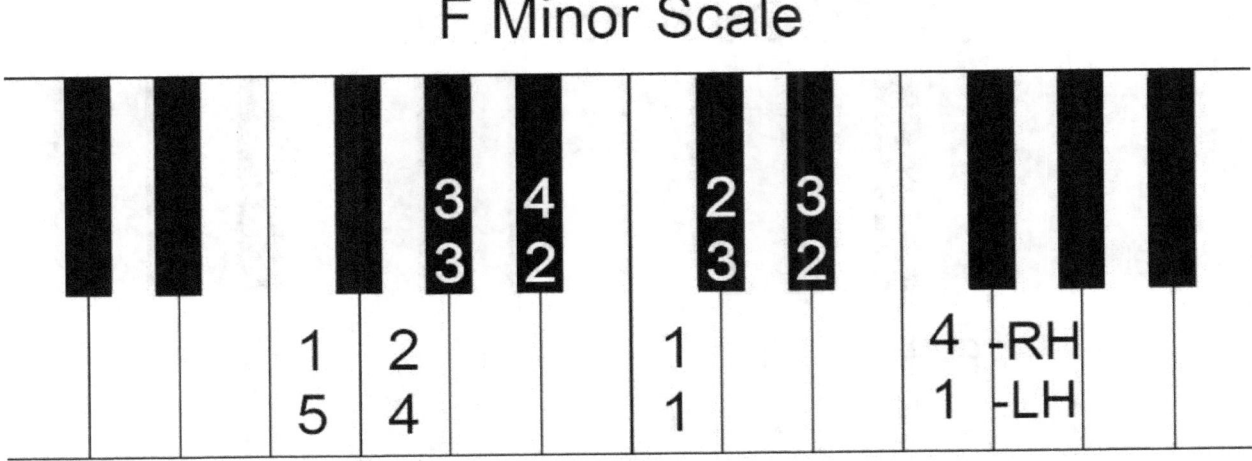

Here are three well-known songs in F minor scale:

- "Symphony No. 40 in G Minor" by Wolfgang Amadeus Mozart
- "The Entertainer" by Scott Joplin
- "All I Ask of You" from The Phantom of the Opera by Andrew Lloyd Webber

F#/Gb Minor Scale

To play the F#/Gb minor scale on the piano, place your right pointer finger on the F#/Gb note, which is the black key to the right of F and the black key to the left of G. Then, follow the pattern of half steps and whole steps: whole, half, whole, whole, half, whole, whole. Play each note in this pattern until you reach the F#/Gb note one octave higher. Remember to use the correct fingerings for each note, which can be found in the piano scale fingering chart.

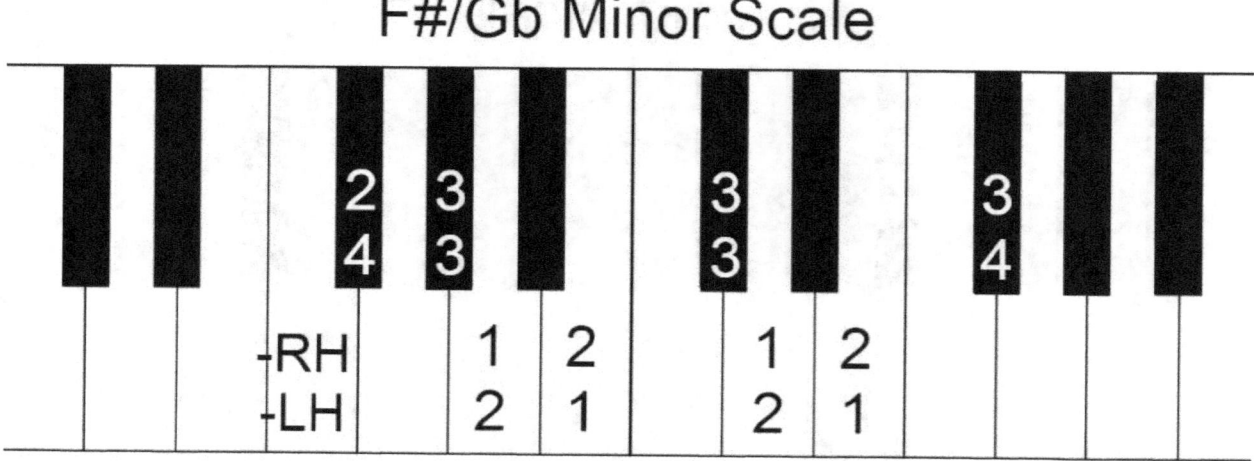

Some popular songs in the F#/Gb minor scale include:

- "Welcome to the Black Parade" by My Chemical Romance
- "Girl on Fire" by Alicia Keys
- "The Final Countdown" by Europe

G Minor Scale

To play the G minor scale on the piano, you'll need to start on the G note and play the notes in sequence. Here are the notes you'll need to play: G, A, Bb, C, D, Eb, and F notes by using all of your fingers. Next, use your middle finger to play the Bb note, followed by your thumb crossing under to the C note. Continue playing the D, Eb, and F notes with your index, middle, and ring fingers, respectively. Finish this off by playing G with your pinky finger. You can also try playing the notes in reverse order, starting with your pinky on G and working your way back, using your thumb, to play to the other G.

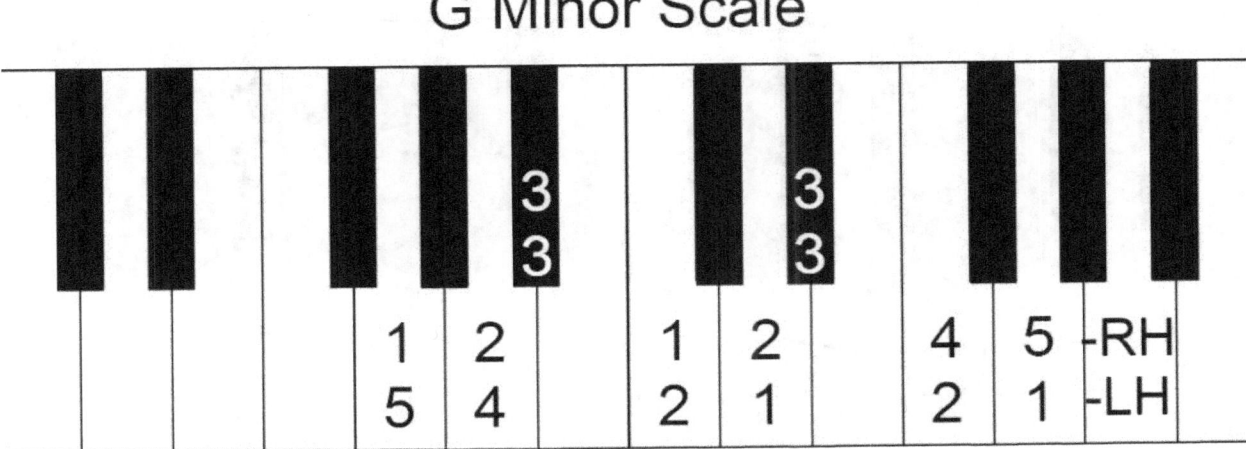

Here are three well-known songs in G minor:

- "Blue (Da Ba Dee)" by Eiffel 65
- "Hungarian Dance No.5 in G Minor" by Johannes Brahms
- "Adagio in G minor" by Tomaso Albinoni

G#/Ab Minor Scale

To play the G#/Ab minor scale on the piano, you will need to use 4 fingers on the right hand and 3 on the left hand. Start with your right middle finger on G#/Ab. From there, use your 4th, 1st, and 2nd fingers to hit the next 3 notes, which are A#/Bb, B, and C#/Db. Then, use your right middle finger to play D#, followed by your thumb to E, and finish out the scale with your index and middle fingers to F# and G#, respectively. Remember to keep your hand relaxed and practice playing the scale slowly at first before building up speed.

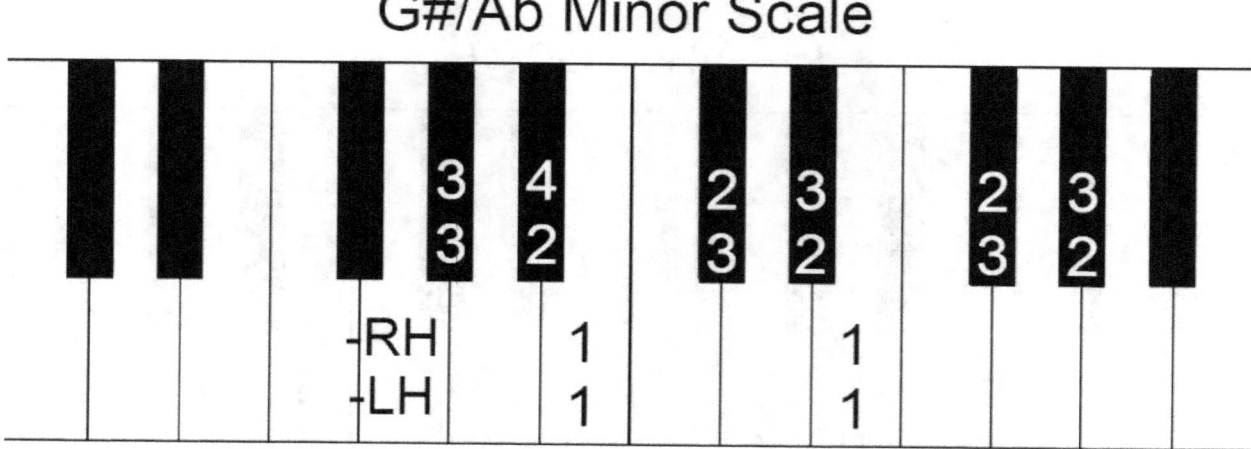

Here are three well-known songs in G#/Ab minor scale:

- "Adagio for Strings" by Samuel Barber
- "Brahms Piano Concerto No. 1" by Johannes Brahms
- "Prelude in G-Sharp Minor" by Sergei Rachmaninoff

RIGHT-HAND MUSICAL PRACTICE

This section is all about practicing music using your right hand. We have some really fun songs for you to try out, like "Mary Had a Little Lamb," "Twinkle Twinkle Little Star," "Hot Cross Buns," "Fuzzy Wuzzy," and "Jingle Bells." These songs have free sheet music that you can print out and use to practice. They are perfect for beginners who are just starting to play the piano. So, let's get started and make some funky music with your right hand!

Mary Had a Little Lamb: Right Hand Only

Let's have a go at playing "Mary Had A Little Lamb" using only your right hand! If you struggle to get the hang of the rhythm, try using a metronome or have someone count out loud while you play!

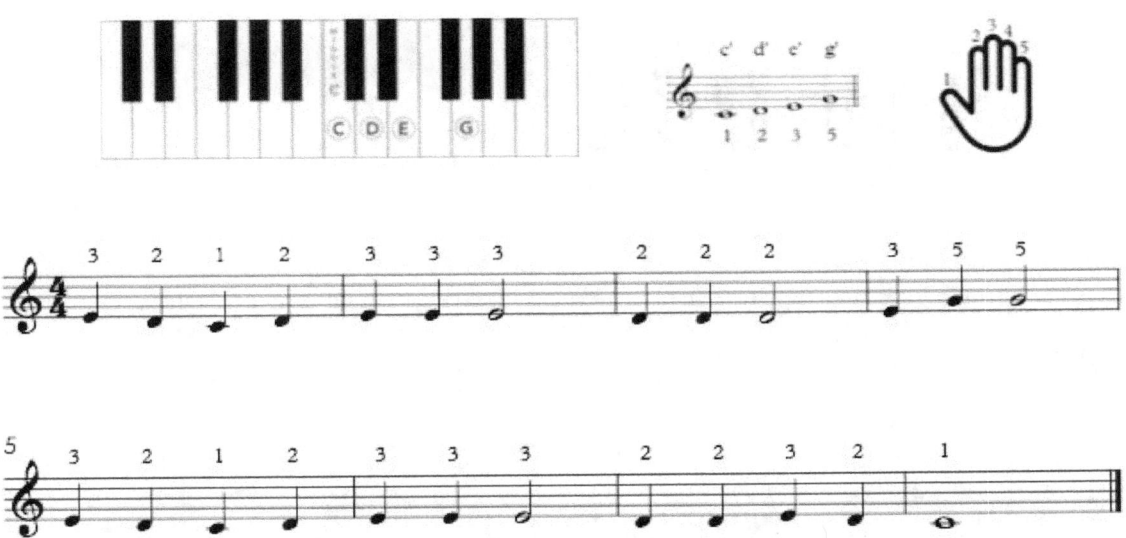

Helpful Hints

- Start by placing your right hand in the correct position. Place your thumb on the note C, which is the white key to the left of the two black keys in the middle of the keyboard.

- Use your other fingers to play the other notes in the song. The first note is E; play this with your middle finger. The second note is D— the white key to the right of C. Play this with your index finger.

- Keep your fingers curved and use the tips of your fingers to press down on the keys. This will help you play more accurately and with better control.

- Try to play each note evenly and with the same amount of pressure. This will help the song sound smoother and more polished.

- Practice each phrase slowly at first, and gradually increase the speed as you get more comfortable with the notes. Remember, practice makes perfect!

Twinkle Twinkle Little Star: Right Hand Only

Ready to try playing "Twinkle Twinkle Little Star" using just your right hand? Let's get playing!

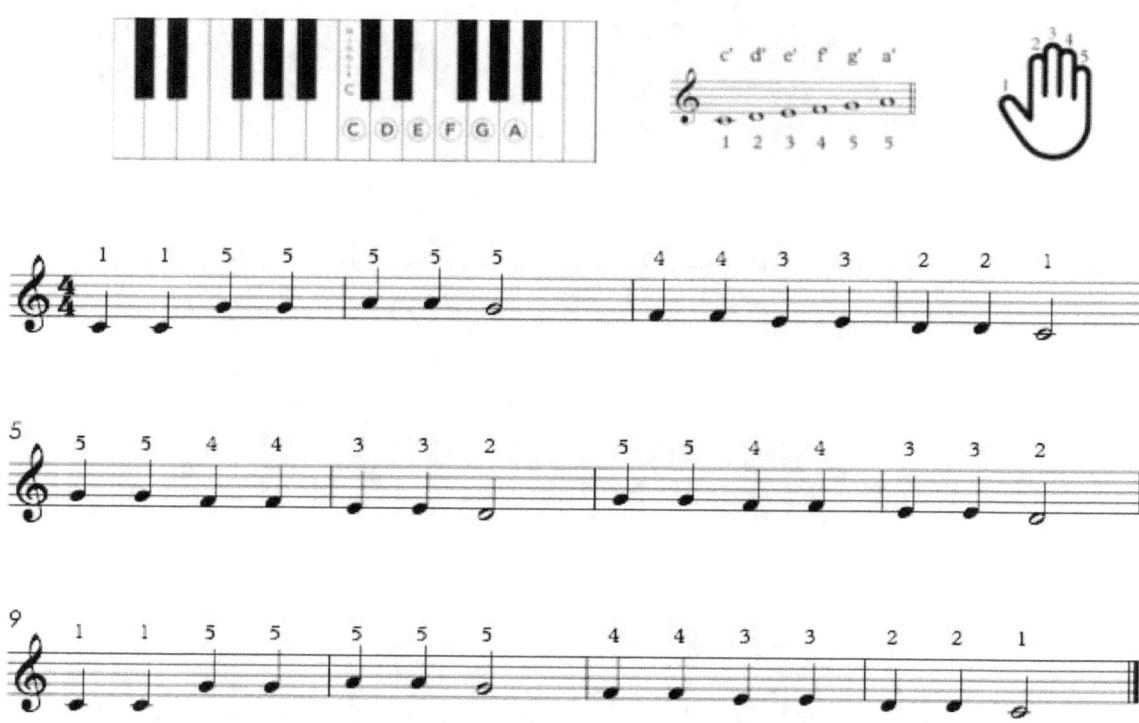

Up for a challenge? Try and sing along as you play!

Helpful Hints

- Start by placing your right thumb on the middle C key (the white key to the left of the two black keys in the middle of the piano).
- Look at the sheet music and find the first note of the song, which is C. Play this note with your thumb.
- Continue to play the notes in the song in order, using your right-hand fingers, as shown in the sheet music. Remember to keep your hand and fingers relaxed as you play.
- Practice playing the song slowly and gradually increase your speed as you become more comfortable.
- Use a metronome or a steady beat to help you keep time as you play.
- Don't be discouraged if you make mistakes! Keep practicing and you'll improve over time.

Hot Cross Buns: Right Hand Only

Ready to try some "Hot Cross Buns" using just your right hand? You can do this!

Hot Cross Buns

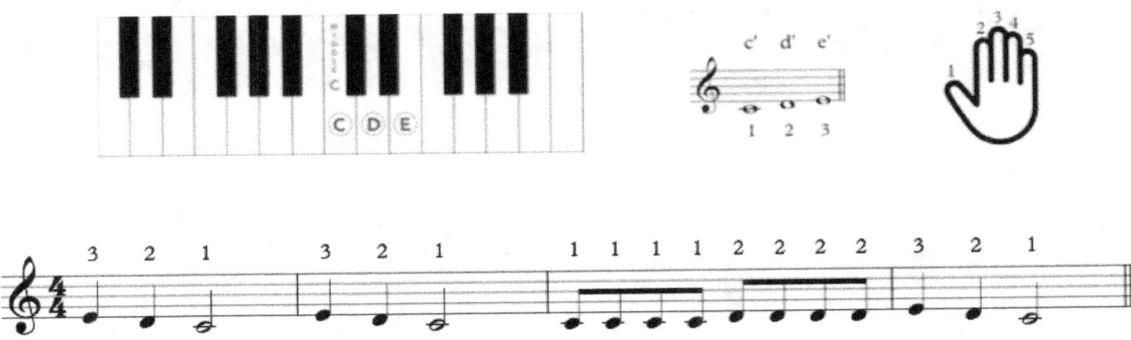

You're doing an amazing job! Soon you'll be playing all of your favorite hits!

Helpful Hints

- First, familiarize yourself with the melody of the song. Listen to a recording or sing the song to yourself before playing it on the piano.

- Place your right hand in the middle of the keyboard with your thumb on middle C. Your other fingers should rest on the keys directly to the right of middle C.
- Follow the sheet music or notes and play the song one note at a time using your right-hand fingers. Start with your right middle finger on the E key to begin this song. Keep your fingers curved and your hand relaxed.
- Pay attention to the rhythm of the song. "Hot Cross Buns" is a simple tune with a basic rhythm, but it's still important to play the notes in the correct timing.
- Practice slowly at first, then gradually increase your speed as you become more comfortable with the song.
- Don't get discouraged if it takes a few tries to get the song right. Remember, practice makes perfect!

Fuzzy Wuzzy: Right Hand Only

Now it's time to try playing "Fuzzy Wuzzy" using only your right hand! Good luck!

Fuzzy Wuzzy

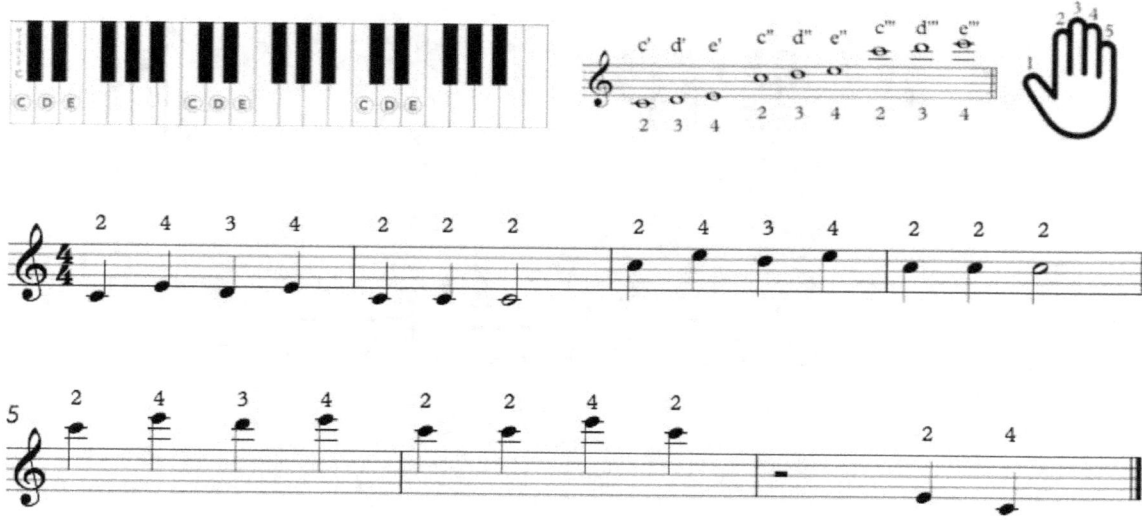

Great job! Learning to use each of your hands on their own to play these songs is so important. That way, when you learn to play songs that need two hands, you won't get confused!

Helpful Hints

- Begin by placing your right index finger on the C note; this one is going to be a little different than the rest!
- With your right hand, play the first note with your index finger, followed by the second note with your right ring finger, then the third note with your middle finger.
- Practice playing the song slowly at first, making sure to use the correct finger positions for each note.
- Once you feel comfortable with the finger positions, try playing the song at a slightly faster tempo, gradually increasing the speed as you improve.

Jingle Bells: Right Hand Only

Feeling festive? Why not give a little show to everybody in your house this Christmas by playing "Jingle Bells"? Spread the festive cheer!

Jingle Bells

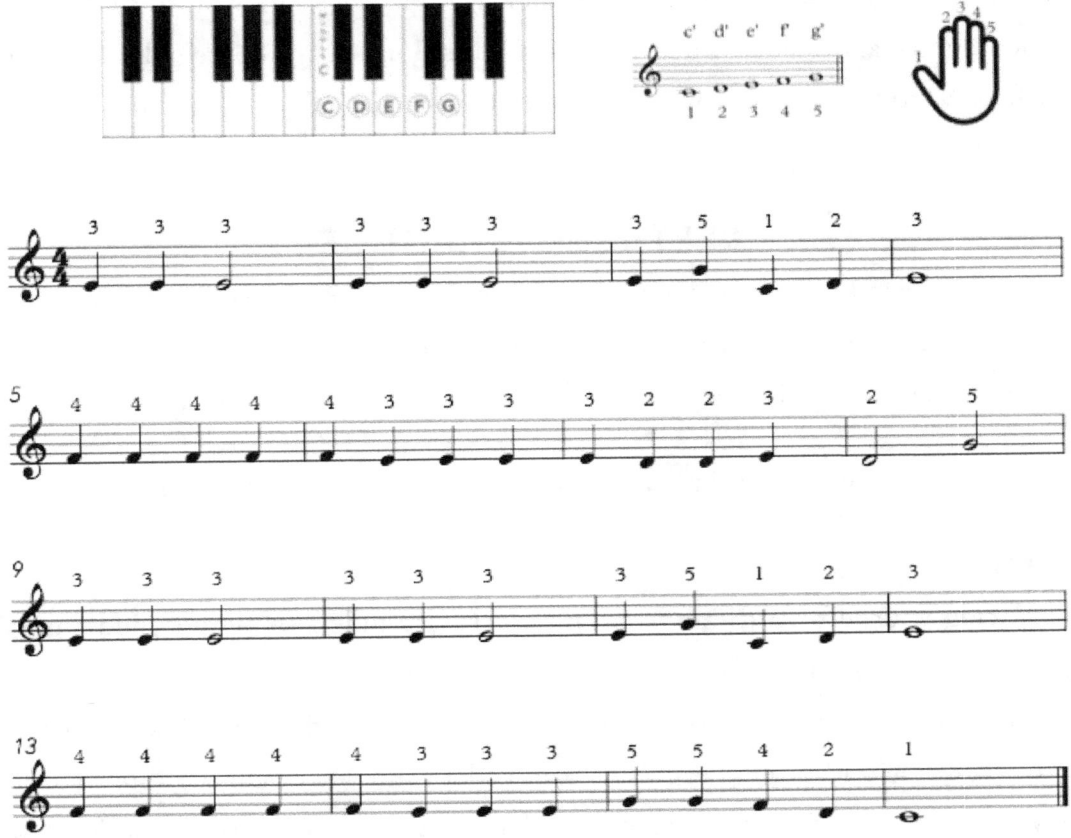

Helpful Hints

- Practice the notes one at a time: Start by playing each note separately with your right hand. This will help you get used to the finger placement and the melody of the song.

- Keep the rhythm: "Jingle Bells" has a catchy rhythm, so it's important to keep that rhythm going as you play. Start slowly and gradually increase your speed as you get more comfortable with the notes.

- Pay attention to the finger numbers: Each note in the song has a corresponding finger number that you should use to play it. Make sure you're using the right finger for each note, as this will help you play the song smoothly and accurately.

- Use the right-hand position: Place your right hand on the piano with your fingers slightly curled, as if holding a small ball. Keep your wrist relaxed and your fingers close to the keys so you can move quickly and easily between notes.

- Practice regularly: Like with any skill, practice is key. Set aside some time each day to practice "Jingle Bells" and focus on the tips mentioned above. Over time, you'll be able to play the song with confidence and ease.

Practicing these songs with only your right hand is a great way for you to build your playing skills. Remember to take it slow, practice regularly, and don't get discouraged if it doesn't sound perfect at first. With practice, you will improve and be able to play these songs with ease. Keep going and have fun with your musical journey!

LEFT-HAND PRACTICE

Are you ready to learn how to use your left hand on the piano? In this section, we will focus on simple and fun exercises to help you develop your left-hand playing skills. You will learn how to coordinate both hands together to make beautiful music. So let's get started!

Here are some awesome left-hand piano exercises that you can try as a beginner:

Finger Exercise

Begin by placing your left-hand thumb on middle C, the index on B, the middle finger on A, the ring finger on G, and the pinky finger on F. Now, lift your pinky finger off the F key and place it back down, then lift your ring finger off the G key and place it back down. Continue this pattern by lifting and placing each finger in order until you reach the thumb again. When you raise your ring finger, you may notice that it's difficult to raise by itself, but don't worry, this is common, and with some practice, you'll get ring finger independence in no time. Then, play the same pattern in reverse.

Chord Practice

Important information! A major chord is comprised of the root, the third, and the fifth notes of the scale. So, a C major chord is made from the use of the C (first or root), E (third note), and G notes (fifth note of the C major scale). While a minor chord is made up of the first, flat third, and fifth of the scale. In the case of C minor, it would be C, Eb, and G. This is the basic formula for major and minor chords, and knowing this will certainly come in handy in the future.

Start by placing your left-hand pinky on C, your left index finger on E, and your thumb on G. Hold the chord for a few seconds, then lift your fingers off the keys and move your hand up to the F Chord, placing your left pinky on F, your index on A and your thumb on C. Repeat the same process, playing the F chord and holding it for a few seconds before moving on to the next chord.

See if you can find all the major and minor chords of all 12 keys. A fun game you can play to help with this is to have a partner say one of the twelve keys with minor or major and see how quickly you can play that chord. For example, your partner will say "A flat major" and you will try to play that chord as quickly as possible. This is a great game to memorize chords and work on your speed.

Arpeggio Exercise

Place your left pinky on middle C, your index finger on E, and your thumb on G. Now, play the C chord by pressing down on the C, E, and G keys at the same time, and then play the notes of the chord one at a time, starting with the C, then the E, and finally the G. Repeat this pattern with other chords, such as the F chord, playing the F, A, and C notes in sequence.

Octave Exercise

Start by placing your left pinky on the lowest C key on your keyboard and your thumb on G. Now, play this chord, then jump up to the next higher C, one octave up, and play the chord there. Once you've played this, jump back to your starting position at the low C on the keyboard. Then jump up two octaves up. Repeat this pattern of starting on the lowest C and skipping to the next octave, and returning to the lowest C after each time you play a higher C. If we numbered the C notes from the left side of the keyboard up, it would go 1, 2, 1, 3, 1, 4, 1, etc. See how far up the keyboard you can go and how fast you can change octaves. You can also do this with the right hand, but instead of starting on the low end of the keyboard, you would start on the high end and repeat the pattern going down the keyboard.

Hand Position Exercise

Begin by placing your left-hand thumb on C, then rest your fingers on the white keys to the left of C, namely B, A, G, and F. Now with your pinky on F, stretch it to E. Hold for a few seconds and bring it back to F. Then do the same to D and bring it back to F. It's okay if your fingers come off the keyboard when you are stretching but make sure to keep that thumb placed on the C key while you stretch; this is home base. Continue this exercise by trying to send your pinky down one note at a time and see how far you can stretch your pinky down the keyboard. This will help your flexibility and range of keys you can reach with your hand. Don't forget to do this with your right hand too! With the right hand, start with C, D, E, F, and G.

Scale Exercise

Let's do a multiple-octave scale exercise! We will use the C scale to go up and down multiple octaves. We will need to use a bit different fingering notation than we used earlier for the C scale. On the left hand, the C scale will be played with the fingers: 5, 4, 3, 2, 1, 3, 2, 1, *4, 3, 2, 1, 3, 2, 1*. The finger notations between the asterisks will be what is repeated as you go up and down the keyboard beyond that first octave. Feel free to make your way back down, with the same fingering but in reverse, when you reach the highest C note with your thumb on your keyboard. This will allow you to easily move up and down the keyboard in this scale across multiple octaves. If you want to try it with the right hand, the fingering notation will look like: 1, 2, 3, 1, 2, 3, 4, 1. You will get this quickly, which will greatly help your dexterity!

Remember, practice is key when it comes to learning the piano. Start with these exercises and try to do them for a few minutes each day. As you get more comfortable with the left hand, you can move on to more advanced exercises and songs.

WHAT DID WE LEARN?

Let's take a look at some of the super cool new things you've learned in this chapter:

- What is a minor scale?
- Can you name one song in the A minor scale?

- How many black keys are in the B minor scale?
- What are some exercises you can do to improve your left-hand piano playing?
- Can you describe how to play the C minor scale?
- How many notes are in the Bb/A# minor scale?
- Name two popular songs in the E minor scale.
- What is the difference between a major scale and a minor scale?
- Describe how to play the F# minor scale on the piano.
- What are the similarities between major scales and minor scales?

Whoa! You've completed another chapter! Well done, you! You've learned about some pretty tough techniques in this chapter, which means you've earned another gold star!

In this chapter, we learned about playing piano using only your right hand. We covered some famous songs you can practice playing with your right hand alone and learned about the different minor scales and how to play them on the piano. Remember, practice makes perfect, so keep working hard!

In the next chapter, we'll explore how to use both hands to play the piano. Playing with two hands may seem a little bit more challenging, but with practice, you'll be able to play even more complex songs! We'll start with some easy exercises to help you get comfortable using both hands and move on to playing some popular songs. Let's get started!

CHAPTER 6:

Piano Mastery Pt. 2—Let Your Fingers Dance!

Beginner Piano Lessons for Kids

Taylor Kent W.

Cool Fact #6: People who learn to play the piano actually use their brains more effectively than people who don't!

When you play the piano, your brain lights up with excitement and uses its superpowers in the most amazing ways!

Playing the piano engages different parts of your brain all at once. Your eyes read the music notes, your ears listen to the melodies, and your fingers tap those magical keys. It's like a symphony of brain activity! All these tasks happening simultaneously make your brain work hard and become more efficient.

But that's not all! Learning to play the piano helps improve other skills too. It boosts your memory power, making it easier for you to remember things like music notes, chords, and even the lyrics to your favorite songs. It also enhances your coordination, as your brain learns to send precise signals to your fingers to hit the right keys at the right time.

So, the next time you sit down at the piano, remember that you're not just making beautiful music; you're also supercharging your brain! You're giving it the ultimate workout and unlocking its hidden powers. Who knows what amazing things you'll be able to accomplish when you use your brain more effectively?

In the previous chapter, you learned how to play the piano using only one hand. Now, it's time to level up and start practicing using two hands at once! Playing with both hands can be challenging, but with practice, you will be able to play beautiful music that sounds like it was played by a professional. In this chapter, we'll introduce you to exercises that will help you train your hands to play together. Let's get started!

THE CHALLENGES OF PLAYING WITH BOTH HANDS

Learning to play piano with both hands can be challenging, but don't worry—everyone struggles at first! Here are some common challenges and tips for overcoming them:

Coordination: It can be difficult to get both hands to play at the same time, especially if you're not used to it.

Tip: Start with simple exercises and take it slow. Practice playing each hand separately first and then gradually try to play them together.

Hand independence: Sometimes, it's hard to get your hands to do different things at the same time.

Tip: Try playing different patterns with each hand. Start with simple songs and work your way up to more complex pieces.

Reading both clefs: When you're reading sheet music, it can be tricky to read and play both the treble and bass clef at the same time.

Tip: Practice reading one hand at a time first. Then, try to read both hands together slowly, one measure at a time.

Different dynamics: Each hand may have to play at different volumes.

Tip: Practice playing scales with one hand loud and the other hand soft, and then switch hands. This will help you get used to playing at different volumes with each hand.

Different rhythms: Each hand may have to play different rhythms, which can be tricky to coordinate.

Tip: Start with simple rhythms and work your way up to more complex ones. Practice each hand separately first and then gradually try to play them together.

Remember, learning to play piano with both hands takes practice and patience. Keep working at it, and you'll get better with time!

WHY IS LEARNING TO PLAY WITH TWO HANDS SO IMPORTANT?

Learning to play piano with both hands is important because it helps you become a well-rounded pianist. Here are some reasons why:

- **Better coordination:** Playing with both hands helps improve coordination between your left and right hands. This means that you can play more complex pieces of music with ease.

- **Increased musicality:** When you play with both hands, you can add more depth and dimension to your music. Your left hand can play bass notes while your right hand plays melodies and harmonies.
- **Versatility:** Once you've mastered playing with both hands, you can play a wider range of music. You'll be able to play classical, pop, jazz, and other genres of music.
- **Professionalism:** Playing with both hands is a fundamental skill that separates amateur and professional pianists. Being able to play with both hands is a sign of professionalism and mastery.

To overcome the challenges of playing piano with both hands, practice regularly and start with simple exercises. Focus on one hand at a time before trying to play both hands together. And don't be afraid to make mistakes—just keep practicing and you'll get better. Remember, learning to play with both hands takes time and patience, but the reward is worth it!

EXERCISE NUMBER ONE

Are you ready to practice your hand independence? This exercise is all about playing with your left and right hands simultaneously. Don't worry; we'll start off easy.

We're going to use the note G for this exercise. Place your right-hand thumb on G, and we'll begin a basic count with your right hand playing on every beat. That means you play on the numbers: 1, 2, 3, 4.

1 and 2 and 3 and 4 and

Next, bring in your left hand with your 5th finger (also on G!) on the 1.

1 and 2 and 3 and 4 and

Now, let's make it a little more challenging. We're going to create different rhythms for each hand. With your left hand, play on the 1, the "and" of the 2, the 3, as well as the "and" after the 4, while continuing to play on the 1, 2, 3, and 4 with your right hand.

This exercise will help you build your rhythm skills and learn how to play with each hand independently. Keep practicing and have fun!

EXERCISE NUMBER TWO

In this exercise, we'll be using both hands to play different notes. Don't worry; it's not as hard as it sounds! We'll be staying in the key of C, which means we'll only be using the white keys.

With your left hand, practice moving from C to G to C (one octave up) and back down. Take your time and get used to the spacing between the keys. Play C with your Left Pinky, G with your index finger, and stretch your hand up the keyboard to play C with your left thumb.

Now, with your right hand (one full octave up from your left hand), play the first five notes of the C scale (C, D, E, F, and G). For every note you play in your left hand, play one in your right hand.

So, your left hand will play: C, G, C, G, C, G, C, G, C. And your right hand will play: C, D, E, F, G, F, E, D, C.

Once you're comfortable with this pattern, try doubling up the speed! Keep practicing and have fun with it! If you have a metronome, it can be helpful to use. It is okay to start slow and work your way up. Starting at 40 beats per minute can be a great place to start.

EXERCISE NUMBER THREE

Are you ready for a challenge? For this exercise, you will start by playing a D major chord on your left hand, with D as the lowest note of the chord to start, playing D, F#, and A with your left pinky, index, and thumb. But don't worry, with some practice and patience, you can do it! With your right hand, play the three notes of a D major chord in ascending and descending order. For example, D, F#, A, A, F#, D. After you finish your descent, change to the next inversion of the D major chord, which is F#, A, and D. Do this using your pinky, middle, and thumb, respectively, following the same ascending and descending pattern of these notes on the right hand. Lastly, do this for the last inversion with A as the lowest note of the chord; you will play this inversion of A, D, F# with your pinky, index, and thumb. Play these same notes in ascending and descending order with your right hand. Then go back down the keyboard to the first inversion with F# as the lowest note, then to the original position while playing the individual notes in ascending and descending order on the right hand. This can become an enjoyable exercise with many benefits for your brain and music skills.

Once you feel comfortable with this, switch the patterns between your hands. Your right hand will play the chord or chord inversion, while your left hand plays the chord's individual notes in ascending and descending order. This might be tricky at first, but with practice, you'll be able to play both patterns at the same time! Feel free to explore this exercise with other major chords!

EXERCISE NUMBER FOUR

Welcome to a new hand independence exercise that will help you improve your piano playing skills! This exercise will focus on playing a two-handed scale but with a twist. You will play the scale with both hands but in different volume levels.

In the first part of the exercise, your right hand will play the scale loudly while your left hand plays it quietly. Then, in the second part of the exercise, you will switch roles: your left hand will play the scale loudly while your right hand plays it quietly. This may feel strange at first, but with practice, you will learn how to bring more feeling and emotion to your piano playing.

This is an important skill to have because it allows you to bring out the melody in a song and make it stand out from the accompaniment. So, let's get started! Play the C major scale with your right hand loud and your left hand quiet. Then, switch to playing the scale with your left hand loud and your right hand quiet. Repeat this pattern a few times and see if you can get the hang of it. After the C major scale, move onto the next major scale until you've made your way through all of them. Happy practicing!

EXERCISE NUMBER FIVE

In this exercise, we'll be playing the C major scale with both hands but with another twist. One hand will play legato, which means smooth and connected, while the other hand will play staccato, which means short and detached. It might seem easy at first, but it's actually quite difficult to coordinate your hands to play different ways at the same time. Don't worry, though; with practice, you'll get the hang of it. Remember, many songs require this kind of coordination, so it's an important skill to develop. Let's get those fingers moving!

Here are the instructions for this exercise:

1. Place your right hand on the higher keys of the piano and your left hand on the lower keys.

2. Starting with your right hand, play the first note of the C major scale legato, which means smooth and connected. Hold down the key for its full value (one beat).

3. At the same time, play the first note of the scale with your left hand staccato, which means short and detached. Tap the key quickly and release it immediately.

4. Continue playing the scale, alternating between legato and staccato with each note. Your right hand will play legato while your left hand plays staccato, and then they will switch.

5. Keep your fingers close to the keys and try to make each note sound distinct and clear.

6. Once you reach the top of the scale, play it in reverse, starting with your left hand playing legato and your right hand playing staccato.

7. As you become more comfortable with the exercise, try increasing the speed while maintaining accuracy and control.

Remember to take your time and practice regularly to develop the necessary hand coordination and control. Good luck!

EXERCISE NUMBER SIX

Have you ever heard of a musical canon? It's when one hand plays a melody, and then the other hand plays the same melody a bit later. Today, we're going to try playing a canon with both of our hands on the piano.

First, we'll start with the right hand playing a tune. Then, the left hand will come in a bar later and play the exact same tune. You can use some of the songs we practiced earlier with one hand and just add the second hand for this exercise!

This exercise may seem easy to understand, but it can be challenging to get it right. You can also do this exercise using the different scales we learned earlier! However, practicing can help you develop the skills you need to play more complex pieces in the future, like Bach's famous Preludes and Fugues. So, let's get started and have fun!

EXERCISE NUMBER SEVEN

Are you ready to challenge your rhythm skills? Our seventh exercise is all about switching up the beat. We'll start with a simple C 5-finger scale, but don't let that fool you—it can get tricky! One hand will be playing steadily, while the other hand will be playing dotted and 8th notes. The 8th notes won't align with the quarter notes, so you'll need to really pay attention to keep the rhythm flowing. If you master this exercise, you can challenge yourself by playing a full octave scale. Let's get started!

Here are the instructions for this exercise:

1. Start by placing your right-hand thumb on middle C and your left pinky on the C one octave below.

2. Play the C 5-finger scale with your right hand (C, D, E, F, G), but use the rhythm pattern: quarter note, dotted quarter note, eighth note, quarter note, quarter note.

3. While your right hand is playing the pattern, your left hand will play the same notes but in quarter notes.

4. Once you've played the scale with your right hand, switch hands and play it with your left hand using the same rhythm pattern.

5. Repeat steps 2–4 several times until you feel comfortable with the rhythm and coordination between your hands.

6. If you want to challenge yourself, try playing a full octave scale using the same rhythm pattern.

Remember to take your time and practice slowly at first. It can be difficult to coordinate your hands with different rhythms, but with practice, you'll be able to master this exercise!

EXERCISE NUMBER EIGHT

Playing chord progressions with both hands is a fun and exciting way to make music on the piano. It can be challenging at first, but with practice, you'll get the hang of it! Here's how you can start:

1. A good one to start with is D minor-G-C. This is a basic jazz chord progression commonly found in jazz songs. If you need a reminder, the notes of these chords are as follows: D minor: D, F, A. G major: G, B, D. And for C major: C, E, G.

2. Begin by playing the chords in a block form with both hands. A block chord is a chord where the notes are all within an octave of each other. Place your left hand on the root note of the chord (D for D minor chord, G for G chord, and C for C chord, etc.) and your right hand on the rest of the notes in the chord. Play the chord with both hands at the same time, making sure all the notes sound together.

3. Once you're comfortable with playing the chords in a block form, try playing them broken up, one note at a time. Use your left hand to play the root note of each chord and your right hand to play the other notes in the chord. You can experiment with different patterns for each hand, but a good one to start with is playing the root note with the left hand and then playing the other notes in the chord with the right hand in a pattern like 1-3-5-3-1.

4. Keep practicing until you can play the chord progressions smoothly and confidently with both hands. As you get more comfortable, try experimenting with different patterns and rhythms.

Remember to take your time and practice regularly. With practice, you'll be able to play chord progressions with both hands like a pro!

EXERCISE NUMBER NINE

Play a simple melody or chord progression with your right hand, and then have your left hand play a different melody or pattern at the same time. This helps with developing hand independence and coordination.

Here are the instructions for this exercise:

1. Choose a simple melody or scale to play with your right hand. You can start with a nursery rhyme or a song that you like.

2. Once you feel comfortable playing the melody with your right hand, try adding your left hand. Your left hand should play a different melody or pattern than your right hand.

3. To start, you can try playing a simple pattern with your left hand, like playing the notes in between the notes of the right-hand melody. You can also try playing a harmony, which means playing notes that sound good with the notes in the right-hand melody. A great place to start doing this, if you are unsure of the key, is to simply play the same notes the right hand is playing. If you explore and play around with this, you may stumble upon a really fun-sounding harmony.

4. Play the melody with your right hand and the pattern or harmony with your left hand at the same time. It may feel tricky at first, but keep practicing!

5. Start slowly and gradually increase your speed as you become more comfortable with the exercise. Remember to practice consistently, and don't get discouraged if it takes some time to get the hang of it.

This exercise is great for developing hand independence and coordination, which are important skills for playing piano. With practice, you'll be able to play more complex pieces with both hands and make beautiful music!

EXERCISE NUMBER TEN

We have some sheet music that has both treble and bass clefs in this book, but if you are looking for more complex pieces, look online for beginner-level pieces with both clefs. Start with easy songs and work your way up to more complex pieces.

Here are some instructions for practicing your sight reading:

1. Find sheet music that has both treble and bass clef. You can ask your piano teacher or look online for beginner-level pieces with both clefs.
2. Start with easy songs and work your way up to more complex pieces.
3. Practice reading the notes for the right hand first, then read the notes for the left hand. Once you are comfortable with both hands separately, try playing them together.
4. Start by playing each hand separately, then slowly try playing them together. It's okay if it's hard at first; take your time and practice slowly. You can use a metronome to help keep a steady tempo.
5. Pay attention to the timing and rhythm of the piece. Make sure both hands are playing at the same speed and in sync with each other.
6. Once you feel comfortable with a piece, try playing it from memory. This will help improve your ability to play both hands together without relying on sheet music.

Remember to take breaks when you need them and practice regularly to improve your skills. Happy playing!

Remember, it's important to start with simple exercises and gradually work your way up to more challenging ones. With practice and patience, you'll be playing with both hands like a pro in no time!

WHAT DID WE LEARN?

You've done a great job! Let's reflect on what we learned in this amazing chapter:

- Why is it important to learn how to play piano with both hands?
- How are major and minor chords composed?
- How can you improve your hand independence and coordination when playing piano with both hands?
- What are some ways you can practice playing piano with both hands?
- What are some challenges you might encounter when playing piano with both hands and how can you overcome them?
- Can you think of any songs you want to learn to play with both hands?

Amazing! You've smashed through yet another chapter and learned how to play piano using both of your hands at once! That's so cool! After all of your hard work, you've earned another gold star!

Great job on learning how to play the piano with both hands! Remember, it's not always easy, but with practice and patience, you can master it.

Now, let's move on to the next chapter, *Music Library*! In this chapter, you will learn about different types of music and how to read sheet music. We will explore different genres of music and learn about famous composers and their works.

You will also get to build your own music library by finding and collecting sheet music of your favorite songs. So get ready to discover new music and have fun playing along!

CHAPTER 7:

A Musical Library!

Beginner Piano Lessons for Kids

Taylor Kent W.

Cool Fact #8: Brigitte Xie, a 3-year-old girl from Connecticut, won an international music competition and got to play at Carnegie Hall!

Winning an international music competition at such a young age is no small feat. It takes dedication, practice, and a whole lot of passion for music. Brigitte's talent and hard work paid off, and she became a shining star, inspiring people of all ages to pursue their dreams and reach for the stars.

Just imagine, you could be like Brigitte too! Who knows, maybe one day you'll be standing on that same stage, captivating the audience with your musical brilliance.

So, keep practicing, keep dreaming, and always believe in yourself. Just like Brigitte, you have the power to make incredible things happen through your love for music. Let your talent soar, and who knows, you might find yourself in the spotlight, playing at the most prestigious venues around the world!

In this chapter, we'll explore a vast collection of sheet music that you can use to hone your piano-playing skills. You'll be able to choose from a variety of pieces that suit your taste and level of skill.

So grab your music stand and let's get ready to rock 'n' roll! Get ready to discover new songs, challenge yourself with harder pieces, and impress your family and friends with your incredible piano-playing skills. The *Musical Library* is here to help you become the best pianist you can be!

LONDON BRIDGE

Are you ready to play a classic nursery rhyme on the piano? "London Bridge" is a song that has been around for centuries and has been sung by generations of children. Now, it's time to learn how to play it on the piano! This catchy tune is perfect for beginners, and it's a great way to practice your piano skills. Let's get started!

London Bridge

Here are some tips on how to play "London Bridge" on the piano with just the right hand:

1. Start by finding the middle C key on your piano. This is the white key just to the left of the two black keys in the middle of the keyboard.

2. The first note of the song is G, which is the white key to the right of the leftmost black key of the group of three black keys. Start this song by pressing down the G key with your middle finger.

3. You will only be using the first four fingers of the right hand and the notes C, D, E, F, G, and A. The finger notation corresponding to the sheet music will look like this on the right hand: 3, 4, 3, 2, 1, 2, 3, 1, 2, 3, 1, 2, 3, 3, 4, 3, 2, 1, 2, 3, 1, 3, 2, 1.

Congratulations! You've just learned how to play "London Bridge" on the piano with your right hand. Practice this pattern until you can play it smoothly and at a comfortable speed.

LIGHTLY ROW

Welcome to the sheet music for "Lightly Row" on piano! This is a delightful and charming folk song that will put a smile on your face. "Lightly Row" is a perfect piece for beginners who are just starting to learn the piano, as it's simple, easy to follow, and enjoyable to play. So let's get started and have fun playing "Lightly Row" on the piano!

Lightly Row

Here are the instructions on how to play "Lightly Row" with just the right hand on the piano:

1. Start by placing your right hand on the piano keys, with your thumb on middle C, which is the white key to the left of the pair of black keys located in the center of the piano.

2. Place your other fingers on the next four white keys to the right of middle C so that your fingers are in order: 2, 3, 4, 5.

3. Since this song only contains the notes of C through G, we won't need to move our right hand much at all!

4. By starting the song with our pinky on G, we can access the rest of the song quite easily.

5. Remember to follow along with the quarter notes and half notes, and with some practice, you will get this down in no time.

And that's it! With a bit of practice, you'll be playing "Lightly Row" on the piano like a pro in no time.

WHEN THE SAINTS GO MARCHING IN

This is a fun and upbeat song you may have heard at a parade or a jazz concert. It's often played on instruments like the trumpet or saxophone, but it sounds great on the piano too!

The song has a catchy melody that you'll love playing with your right hand while your left hand keeps a steady beat with the chords. You might notice that the song has a swing rhythm, which means that some of the notes are held a little longer than others to create a bouncy feel.

Don't worry if it takes a little bit of practice to get the hang of the swing rhythm—it's a common feature in jazz and blues music, and it's great to start developing your sense of rhythm early on. Once you've got the hang of it, you'll be playing "When the Saints Go Marching In" like a pro!

When The Saints Go Marching In

Here are the instructions on how to play "When the Saints Go Marching In" with just the right hand on the piano:

1. Start with your right hand in the middle of the piano, with your thumb (1) resting on the middle C note.
2. Practice playing the notes slowly at first, and then try to speed up as you get more comfortable with the song.
3. Sing along or hum the tune as you play to help you keep the rhythm.

Remember to have fun and keep practicing!

BINGO

Are you ready to learn a new song on the piano? First, we're going to play "Bingo," a classic children's song that's sure to get you tapping your toes and singing along. This sheet music has all the notes you need to play the song with both hands, so get ready to put your new skills to the test. Let's get started!

Bingo

Here are some instructions on how to play "Bingo" with just the right hand on the piano:

1. Start by finding the C note one octave up from middle C.
2. The first line of the song goes like this: "There was a farmer had a dog, and Bingo was his name-o"."

Remember to take it slow at first, and practice playing each note with the right finger. With a little practice, you'll be able to play "Bingo" with ease. Good luck!

YANKEE DOODLE

Let's learn how to play "Yankee Doodle" on the piano. This is a classic tune that you might have heard before, and now you get to play it with both hands! Get ready to march along and play this patriotic song on the piano.

Yankee Doodle

Here are tips on how to play "Yankee Doodle" with just the right hand on the piano:

1. Start by placing your right hand on the piano keys.
2. Find the C note, one octave above middle C.
3. This song contains the notes E through F, which is a rather big range of notes. By starting with your thumb on G, you can easily maneuver through the wide range of notes within this song.

Congratulations! You've just played "Yankee Doodle" with your right hand on the piano. Keep practicing and you'll be able to play even more songs in no time!

BROTHER JOHN

Are you ready to learn a new song on the piano? This one is called "Brother John." It's a catchy melody that you might have heard before. You'll be playing with both hands, using the notes you've learned so far. The song is made up of simple patterns, but don't let that fool you! It can be tricky to play smoothly and in time. With practice and patience, you'll be able to play "Brother John" like a pro! So let's go and start playing this fun tune on the piano.

Brother John

Here are the instructions on how to play "Brother John" with just the right hand on the piano:

1. Start by placing your right-hand thumb on the middle C note, which is located in the middle of the piano keyboard.

2. The first note of "Brother John" is C. Place your second finger (index finger) on the D note, which is the white key located to the right of the middle C.

3. Next, place your third finger (middle finger) on the E note, which is located to the right of the D note.

4. When it comes time to play F use your fourth finger (ring finger) to play this key.

5. Finally, when the G note comes, place your fifth finger on the key, which is the white key located to the right of the F note.

6. Now that your fingers are in position, it's time to play the song. The melody for "Brother John" goes like this:

"Are you sleeping, Are you sleeping?" (play C D E C, C D E C)

"Brother John, Brother John," (play E F G, E F G)

"Morning bells are ringing, morning bells are ringing." (play G A G F E C, G A G F E C)

Repeat the melody a few times until you get the hang of it. Remember to use the correct finger for each note and to keep your fingers curved and relaxed while playing.

Congratulations! You just learned how to play "Brother John" on the piano with just your right hand. Keep practicing to get better and try playing with both hands once you feel comfortable.

THIS OLD MAN

Get ready to learn a catchy tune that will have you tapping your toes and humming along in no time. Children have enjoyed this song for generations, and now it's your turn to bring it to life on the piano. So, let's dive in and start playing "This Old Man"!

This Old Man

Here are the instructions on how to play "This Old Man" with just the right hand on piano:

1. Find the middle C on your piano.
2. Put your second finger (finger 2) on the next white key to the right of C. This is the note D.
3. Put your third finger (finger 3) on the next white key to the right of D. This is the note E.
4. Put your fourth finger (finger 4) on the next white key to the right of E. This is the note F.
5. Put your fifth finger (finger 5) on the next white key to the right of F. This is the note G.
6. Now, let's play the song! Since this song's lowest note is middle C, we can start with our thumb there, and with the highest note being A, we won't have to move our fingers much!
7. Sing the words to the song as you play: "This old man, he played one, he played knick-knack on my thumb, with a knick-knack paddywhack, give a dog a bone, this old man came rolling home!"

Practice playing the song slowly at first, and then try to speed it up a bit as you get more comfortable with the finger positions.

LONG, LONG AGO

Welcome to another exciting piece in our music library! Here, we have "Long, Long Ago," a beautiful melody that will transport you to a different time and place. This song is like a musical time machine that will take you on a journey through the ages. With its soothing notes and gentle rhythms, you'll feel relaxed and at peace. This piece is perfect for anyone who loves to play the piano. So sit back, relax, and let's dive into "Long, Long Ago."

Long, Long Ago

Here are instructions on how to play "Long, Long Ago" with just the right hand on piano:

1. Start with your right hand in the middle of the piano.
2. Place your thumb on middle C.
3. Play the notes C, C, D, E, E, and F. These make up the first measure or bar of this song.
4. The second bar is made up of the notes G, A, G, and E.
5. The third bar consists of the notes G, F, E, and D.
6. The fourth measure is as follows: F, E, D, and C.

Congratulations! You have played "Long, Long Ago" with just your right hand. Remember to practice slowly at first and gradually increase your speed as you become more comfortable with the notes. Happy playing!

BILLY BOY

Welcome to the sheet music for "Billy Boy" on piano! This is a fun and upbeat folk song that will get your fingers tapping and your feet moving. With this sheet music, you can learn to play this classic tune on the piano and impress your friends and family with your musical skills. "Billy Boy" is a popular song that has been enjoyed by generations of people, and now it's your turn to play it too. So grab your piano and get ready to have some fun with this catchy melody!

Billy Boy

Here are the instructions on how to play "Billy Boy" with just the right hand on piano:

1. Put your right thumb on the note C.
2. Since this song starts on E, you can start playing this song with your thumb on E to the right of middle C.
3. Now that we have a few songs under our belt, this one should come rather easily. The lowest note is B, just to the left of middle C, and the highest note is C, which is a whole octave above middle C. You may need to stretch and move your hands a bit for this one, but it is sure to feel great once you get it.

Remember to take your time and practice each step slowly and carefully before moving on to the next. Good luck and have fun playing "Billy Boy" on the piano!

FARMER IN THE DELL

Welcome to another exciting piece of sheet music in our music library for piano players! Here, we have "Farmer In The Dell," a traditional nursery rhyme that dates back to the 19th century. The song has a quick tempo, known as Allegro, which means it should be played at a fast pace. Don't worry if it takes a bit of time to get used to playing it quickly, though—with practice, you'll be able to master it in no time! So, grab your sheet music and get ready to play this classic tune on the piano!

Farmer in the Dell

Here are the instructions on how to play "Farmer In The Dell" with just the right hand on the piano:

1. Start with your right-hand thumb on middle C.
2. "Farmer In The Dell" doesn't have a large variety of notes, but this one will test your finger mobility, stretching, and hand movement. With some practice, you'll learn how to keep your fingers from tangling up and hitting all the right notes on time.

Congratulations! You have played "Farmer In The Dell" using your right hand on the piano. Remember to take it slow and practice each hand separately at first.

CLEMENTINE

Welcome to the sheet music for "Clementine." This is a classic folk song that is perfect for piano players of all levels. The melody is catchy and fun to play, and it features some exciting Allegro sections that will challenge your fingers and make you feel like a true pianist. Get ready to tap your feet and hum along as you play this cheerful tune on the piano!

Clementine

Here are the instructions on how to play "Clementine" with just the right hand on piano:

1. Find the middle C on your piano.
2. Now place your thumb on middle C.
3. Start by playing the F key with your ring finger.
4. There isn't a huge variety of differentiating notes in this song. After playing the first middle C in the notation, you may want to move your hand up the keys to play the other notes easier. This song will require you to move around a bit, but in the end, it is only going to make you that much better at the piano!

Congratulations, you just played "Clementine" with your right hand on the piano!

ROW YOUR BOAT

Are you ready to row your boat down the musical stream? "Row Your Boat" is a classic nursery rhyme you can play on the piano. With simple melodies and repetitive lyrics, this song is a great way to practice your piano skills. You can play it slowly or quickly, depending on your level of expertise. Don't forget to use your right and left hands together for the full effect! So grab your oars and get ready to row your way to musical success.

Row Your Boat

Here are the instructions on how to play "Row Your Boat" with just the right hand on piano:

1. First, locate the middle C on your keyboard.
2. Next, find the first F key to the right of middle C.
3. Now start the song by playing the first note, F, with your thumb.
4. Because this song contains two different F keys, you will need to learn how to move your hands quickly and accordingly.
5. Don't forget about the dotted half notes!

Congratulations, you have just played "Row Your Boat" with your right hand on the piano! Keep practicing to get even better.

THE MULBERRY BUSH

This traditional English nursery rhyme is a fun and upbeat tune that is sure to get you tapping your feet. With its catchy melody and playful lyrics, this song is a great way to learn how to play piano. So grab your sheet music, get ready to play, and let's learn how to play "The Mulberry Bush" on piano!

The Mulberry Bush

Here are the instructions on how to play "The Mulberry Bush" with just the right hand on piano:

1. Find the Middle C on your piano.
2. Place your right hand's thumb (your number 1 finger) on the note F.
3. Next, use your middle finger (your number 3 finger) on the note A.
4. Don't be afraid to get your pinky involved; use this, your number 5 finger, to hit the higher C.

That's it! You've just played "The Mulberry Bush" with your right hand on the piano. Keep practicing to get faster and smoother at playing this tune. Good luck!

HAPPY BIRTHDAY

Are you ready to learn how to play one of the most famous songs in the world on the piano? That's right; we're talking about "Happy Birthday"! This classic tune is a must-know for any aspiring pianist, and it's perfect for celebrating birthdays and other special occasions. So grab your party hat and let's get started!

Happy Birthday

Here are the instructions on how to play "Happy Birthday" with just the right hand on piano:

1. Start by placing your right-hand thumb on the middle C key.
2. Start by playing the first two notes of the song, the C note, with your thumb.
3. Now, continue to play the notes with the natural fingering the fingers fall on by having your thumb on middle C.
4. When it comes time to play the higher C, play this with your pinky, this will require you to either stretch or move your hand.

Congratulations! You have just played the right-hand part of "Happy Birthday."

Practice playing the song slowly at first, then try to speed up. You can also try adding some dynamics to make the song more expressive, such as playing some notes louder or softer than others. Keep practicing, and soon you'll be able to play "Happy Birthday" like a pro!

WE WISH YOU A MERRY CHRISTMAS

Are you excited for the holiday season? Get ready to play the cheerful tune of "We Wish You a Merry Christmas" on your piano! This popular holiday song is loved by people of all ages, and it's a great way to spread joy and happiness during the festive season. Don't worry if it seems difficult at first; with practice and patience, you'll be able to master it in no time. Let's get started and spread some holiday cheer with "We Wish You a Merry Christmas" on the piano!

We Wish You a Merry Christmas

Here are the instructions on how to play "We Wish You a Merry Christmas" with just the right hand on piano:

1. Start with your right-hand thumb (finger number 1) on middle C.
2. Remember to play each note with the correct finger and use the right amount of pressure.
3. Keep the rhythm steady and even throughout the song.
4. Congratulations, you've just learned how to play "We Wish You a Merry Christmas" on the piano with your right hand!

Remember to practice slowly at first and gradually increase your speed. Happy playing!

THE MUFFIN MAN

Welcome to the sheet music for "The Muffin Man" on piano! This classic nursery rhyme tells the story of a friendly baker who lives on Drury Lane. Get ready to sing along as you play the tune on your piano!

The Muffin Man

Here are the instructions on how to play "The Muffin Man" with just the right hand on piano:

1. Start by finding middle C.
2. Find the D key next to middle C.
3. Place your thumb on D; this is where you will start the song.
4. Remember to watch for the dotted notes!
5. That's it! You've played "The Muffin Man." Try playing it a few more times to get the hang of it.

Remember to keep a steady beat while playing and practice slowly at first before gradually increasing your speed. Have fun playing "The Muffin Man" on the piano!

ALOUETTE

Are you ready to learn a new song on the piano? Now we will introduce you to "Alouette," a fun and catchy tune that originates from France. This song is great for practicing your piano skills, especially when it comes to using both hands to play different notes. "Alouette" is played at a moderate tempo, which means you can take your time to learn and practice each note. In this song, you will find a combination of different notes, so get ready to use all your music skills! So let's get started and play "Alouette" on the piano!

Alouette

Here are the instructions on how to play "Alouette" with just the right hand on piano:

1. The lowest note of this song is D, just to the right of middle C, while the highest note is D, one octave up.
2. By placing your thumb on G, you will have a great place to start playing this song.
3. If you know the song lyrics, sing along and try to match the notes you play on the keyboard to the melody!

Remember to practice slowly at first and gradually increase your speed as you get more comfortable with the song. Keep practicing until you can play the song smoothly and confidently!

ODE TO JOY

Welcome to the sheet music for "Ode to Joy"! This song is one of the most well-known pieces of classical music ever written, composed by Ludwig van Beethoven. "Ode to Joy" is a joyful and uplifting melody that is often played on special occasions, such as graduations and weddings. It features a variety of musical techniques and dynamics, from soft and slow to loud and fast. Playing this song on the piano is not only fun, but it can also help improve your finger dexterity and hand-eye coordination. So, get ready to experience the joy of playing "Ode to Joy" on the piano!

Ode to Joy

Here are instructions on how to play "Ode to Joy" with just the right hand on piano:

1. Find middle C on your keyboard.
2. The lowest note of this song is D, just to the right of middle C.
3. Start by placing your thumb on D.
4. This song won't require you to move your hand much, but remember to watch for those dotted notes!

Congratulations! You just played "Ode to Joy" on the piano with just your right hand!

O CHRISTMAS TREE

Welcome to the section on "O Christmas Tree"! This is a classic holiday song that's sure to get you in the festive spirit. "O Christmas Tree" is a German carol that's been translated into English, and it's played all over the world during the holiday season. The melody is beautiful and the lyrics are heartwarming, making it a great choice to play on the piano for your family and friends. So get ready to spread some holiday cheer with "O Christmas Tree"!

O Christmas Tree

Here are some tips on how to play "O Christmas Tree" with just the right hand on piano:

1. Start by placing your thumb on the D note next to middle C.
2. The highest note in this song is E.
3. This may require stretching your hands and learning to move in time with the song.
4. Don't worry, though. With some practice, you'll get it in no time, and you'll be able to play this song just in time for the holidays!

Congratulations! You have just learned how to play "O Christmas Tree" with just your right hand on the piano. Keep practicing and have fun making beautiful music!

OH SUSANNA

"O Susanna" is a fun and lively song that you'll love playing on the piano! It tells the story of a man traveling to New Orleans to see his love, Susanna. This song is perfect for beginners who want to practice playing with both hands.

With a bouncy rhythm and catchy melody, "O Susanna" is a great way to practice your piano skills. And once you get the hang of it, you'll be able to play it with ease and confidence!

So get ready to play this fun and exciting song on the piano. With practice and dedication, you'll be able to master it in no time!

Oh, Susanna

Here are the instructions to play "Oh Susanna" with just the right hand on piano:

1. Start by placing your thumb on D.
2. This song has a wider range of different beats, so make sure to watch for those various dotted notes!

Congratulations, you have just played "Oh Susanna" on the piano with your right hand! Keep practicing to improve your skills and play more songs.

TEN LITTLE INDIANS

Welcome, young pianists, to another exciting section of our *Music Library*! Now, we are going to learn to play the popular song "Ten Little Indians" on the piano. This song is a fun and catchy tune that you will enjoy playing. It's a great song to practice playing with both hands, and it will help you improve your finger dexterity. So let's put on our thinking caps, sit at the piano, and get ready to play "Ten Little Indians"!

Ten Little Indians

Here are some tips to play "Ten Little Indians" on Piano, and now we are going to start getting the left hand involved!

1. This song starts with the right hand on middle C.

2. This song is a great place to start incorporating the left hand, as you will only be using one hand at a time.

3. Try to play the song smoothly and evenly, with the same amount of pressure on each note. Remember to keep your fingers curved and your wrists relaxed.

4. Once you feel comfortable playing the song with both hands, you can try playing it at different tempos (speeds) to make it sound faster or slower. You can also experiment with playing the notes louder or softer to create different dynamics.

5. With practice, you'll be able to play "Ten Little Indians" with both hands like a pro!

MY BONNIE

This is a fun and easy song to play that everyone will recognize. The melody of "My Bonnie" is catchy and you can impress your friends and family by playing it on the piano. With this sheet music, you'll learn how to play the song step-by-step, and soon you'll be playing "My Bonnie" like a pro!

My Bonnie

Here are some tips on how to play "My Bonnie" with both hands on the piano:

1. Let's ramp up the difficulty with the left hand.

2. Remember, if you need help with the left-hand notes, the diagram in Chapter 4 is a great reminder!

3. One way to place your hands to start this song is with your right-hand thumb on D to the right of middle C and your left-hand pointer finger on G to the left of middle C.

4. You may need to move both hands a bit to play this, but you will surely get it with practice!

5. After you play the last note, lift your hands off the piano and take a deep breath. You did it!

Remember to practice slowly at first and gradually increase your speed as you become more comfortable with the song. Happy playing!

AMAZING GRACE

In this section, we will explore the beautiful song "Amazing Grace" and its sheet music for piano. "Amazing Grace" is a beloved song with a rich history, and it is often played at important events and celebrations.

So, get ready to experience the beauty and power of "Amazing Grace" through the magic of piano music. Let's dive into the world of this wonderful song and learn how to play it with all the passion and emotion it deserves!

Amazing Grace

Here are some suggestions on how to play "Amazing Grace" with both hands on the piano:

1. Start by playing the D note to the right of middle C with your thumb.
2. Then, by placing your left thumb on B to the left of middle C, you can start playing with the left hand.
3. Remember to watch for the specific beats with each hand.
4. By practicing each line separately with the proper beats, you will then be able to play them smoothly, and it will be easier to play the whole song together with both hands!

Congratulations, you've learned how to play "Amazing Grace" with both hands on the piano! Keep practicing to improve your skills and have fun playing music!

CRADLE SONG

Welcome to the sheet music for "Cradle Song"! This gentle lullaby is perfect for playing on the piano to soothe a little one to sleep. The piece has a slow and peaceful tempo, making it easy to play and listen to. In this sheet music, you'll find the notes for both the right and left hands, so you can play the melody and accompaniment at the same time. Get ready to create a tranquil and peaceful sound with "Cradle Song" on the piano.

Cradle Song

Here are instructions on how to play "Cradle Song" with both hands on the piano:

1. Sit at the piano and place your hands on the keys with your fingers curved and relaxed.
2. The right hand will play the melody and the left hand will play the accompaniment.
3. Start with your left thumb on G to the left of middle C.
4. Place your left pinky on C, the C one octave down from middle C.

Congratulations, you just played "Cradle Song" with both hands on the piano! Keep practicing and soon you'll be playing even more songs.

DECK THE HALLS

Welcome to another classic Christmas song that piano players of all ages love to play: "Deck the Halls"! This festive tune is perfect for spreading joy during the holiday season. With its catchy melody and lively rhythm, you'll be singing along in no time. Get ready to play some jolly notes on the piano and feel the spirit of the holidays fill your heart!

Deck The Halls

Here are the instructions on how to play "Deck The Halls" with both hands on the piano:

1. Start by placing your right hand on the piano, with your thumb on middle C.
2. By placing your left-hand thumb on A to the left of middle C, we have a great placement to start the show!
3. Remember to watch the beats!
4. Feel free to sing along to help your melody.
5. If you need to, practice with one hand at a time and then together. This can help make great building blocks to get the foundation of the song.

Congratulations, you have now learned how to play "Deck The Halls" on the piano with both hands!

AULD LANG SYNE

Are you ready to learn a new song on the piano? Let's welcome the New Year with "Auld Lang Syne"! This beautiful Scottish melody has become a popular tune all around the world, especially during New Year's Eve celebrations. It's a song that encourages us to cherish the memories we've made, even as we move forward into the future. "Auld Lang Syne" has a lovely and simple melody that's easy to learn, but it's full of feeling and emotion. Playing it on the piano is a great way to share the joy of the holiday season with your friends and family. So let's get started and learn how to play this wonderful song together!

Auld Lang Syne

Here are instructions on how to play "Auld Lang Syne" with both hands on the piano:

1. Find middle C.
2. Start by placing your right thumb on G to the right of middle C.
3. Place your left thumb on G to the left of middle C.
4. From these hand positions, you can start to play the tune!
5. Finally, sing along with the tune! "Should old acquaintance be forgot, and never brought to mind? Should old acquaintance be forgot, and days of auld lang syne?"

DING DONG BELL

Welcome to the sheet music for "Ding Dong Bell"! This is a fun and playful song that you can learn to play on the piano. The song has a catchy tune and will have you tapping your feet in no time. It's a great song to practice your piano skills and learn how to play with both hands. "Ding Dong Bell" is a traditional nursery rhyme that has been enjoyed by children for generations. In this sheet music, you will find notes and instructions on how to play the song on the piano. So grab your piano and get ready to play "Ding Dong Bell"!

Ding Dong Bell

Here are some tips on how to play "Ding Dong Bell" with both hands on the piano:

1. Start with your right-hand thumb on middle C.
2. Place your left-hand thumb on G to the left of middle C.
3. The beats in this song may feel strange, but by practicing one hand at a time, you will have it with ease.
4. Remember to take it slow to have a good foundation to build on, and celebrate each small success you make!

Congratulations, you have played "Ding Dong Bell" on the piano with both hands!

ROCK-A-BYE BABY

Are you ready to sing a lullaby to the little ones? Then get ready to learn how to play "Rock-a-Bye Baby" on the piano! This classic tune is perfect for soothing babies to sleep, and now you can add your own gentle touch with the beautiful sound of the piano. With its simple melody, this song is perfect for beginners. So get comfy, sit at your piano, and let's learn how to play "Rock-a-Bye Baby"!

Rock-a-Bye, Baby

Here are the instructions on how to play "Rock-a-Bye Baby" with both hands on piano:

1. Let's ramp up the difficulty!
2. We are going to introduce chords into the left hand.
3. Practice one hand at a time playing the song first; with something new like this, it can really help.
4. Start by placing your right-hand thumb on A to the right of middle C.
5. Place your left-hand thumb on middle C and your left pinky on F.
6. From here, you have a great hand position to start playing.
7. Feel free to sing the lyrics as you play to help get the hang of it.
8. The lyrics go as such "Rock a bye baby, on the tree top, when the wind blows, the cradle will rock. When the bough breaks, the cradle will fall, And down will come baby, cradle and all.
9. Practice playing the song slowly at first, and then gradually increase your speed as you get more comfortable.

That's it! Have fun playing "Rock-a-Bye Baby" on the piano with both hands.

SILENT NIGHT

"Silent Night" is a beautiful and peaceful Christmas carol that is loved by many. It is a song that brings joy during the holiday season. This song is often played on the piano and has a slow and gentle melody. The words of the song talk about the birth of Jesus and the happiness and peace that he brings to the world. When playing this song on the piano, it is important to play each note with care and attention, creating a soft and soothing sound. Get ready to experience the calming and joyful atmosphere of "Silent Night" as you play it on the piano.

Silent Night

We are going to add a lot more difficulty with this one. Here are some step-by-step instructions on how to play "Silent Night" on the piano with both hands with more complex chords on the left hand.

1. Start with your right thumb on E to the right of middle C.
2. Place your left-hand thumb on G to the left of middle C.
3. The left hand will start at the same time the right-hand plays G, by playing a C major chord.
4. This first C major chord will use the left-hand pinky on C, middle finger on E, and thumb on G.
5. This song will test you, but by mastering it, your skill to read, play chords and melodies at the same time, and play beautiful music will be exponentially higher!
6. Remember to practice one hand at a time first to get a good foundation.

Repeat these steps to play the entire song. Remember to play the notes at the right time and keep a steady beat!

DANNY BOY

Welcome to the last sheet music song, "Danny Boy"! This is a beautiful and classic Irish melody that you're sure to enjoy playing on the piano. The song is often sung at special occasions, such as weddings and funerals, and has been popular for many years. The music is written in a gentle and flowing style, with some notes that rise and fall gracefully. You'll love the sound of the melody as you play it on the piano. So let's get started and have some fun learning this wonderful song!

Danny Boy

Here are the instructions to play "Danny Boy" with both hands on the piano:

1. Start by placing your right-hand thumb on B to the left of middle C.

2. Get your left hand ready to play a C major chord with your thumb on G; this will get you ready to start the song.

3. When the second chord with the left hand comes in, you can play it with your left pinky on C and your thumb moves from G to F.

4. By the time the fourth chord comes around on the left hand, simply move your pinky and middle finger down a single note, so from C major (C, E, G), move to B, D, and G, which is a G major inversion! Isn't that exciting?

5. If you need to, practice the song with one hand at a time, first the right hand for the melody and then the left hand for the chords, this will make it that much easier when you play them together.

6. Then practice playing both hands together, using the right hand to play the melody and the left hand to play the accompaniment.

7. Keep practicing until you can play the song with confidence.

Congratulations! You've just learned how to play "Danny Boy" with both hands on the piano.

WHAT DID WE LEARN?

What was your favorite part of this chapter? With so many wonderful songs to learn to play, you'll be giving mini concerts in no time at all!

- Which song is your favorite?
- Which song was the most difficult to play?
- Can you name all of the songs that use Allegro?
- Which song was the easiest to play?

Another end of the chapter already? You know what that means! You've earned another fantastic gold star! Well done, young pianist! You've earned quite the collection of stars now!

And that concludes our musical library chapter! We hope you enjoyed playing the different songs we gathered for you to learn on the piano. Remember, practice makes perfect, so keep playing and have fun exploring the world of music. Whether you're playing a classic tune or creating your own melody, music is a wonderful way to express yourself and share your feelings with others. So, keep on playing and stay tuned for more exciting adventures in the world of music!

BONUS:

Flashcards

Beginner Piano Lessons for Kids

Taylor Kent W.

Welcome to the Bonus Chapter on Flashcards! Here, you'll find an exciting new way to practice and learn about music.

In this chapter, you'll discover a variety of flashcards that are specially designed for young pianists. They are easy to use, cut out, and fun to help expand your music theory skills. You can use them to test your knowledge of music theory or even play games with your friends.

No matter how good your music theory skills are, these flashcards will help you take them to the next level. So, let's get started and have some fun with music flashcards!

TEMPO AND DYNAMICS

Largo 40-60 BPM	Slow and Steady! Imagine a tortoise or a snail!
Andante 76-108 BPM	Medium Speed! Think about a steady walking pace!
Allegro 120-168 BPM	Nice and speedy! Like a cheetah or a race car!
P is for Piano	Quiet as a mouse!
M is for Mezzo	A little bit quiet or loud! In the middle!
F is for Forte	Loud like a rocket ship!

NOTES ON THE TREBLE STAFF

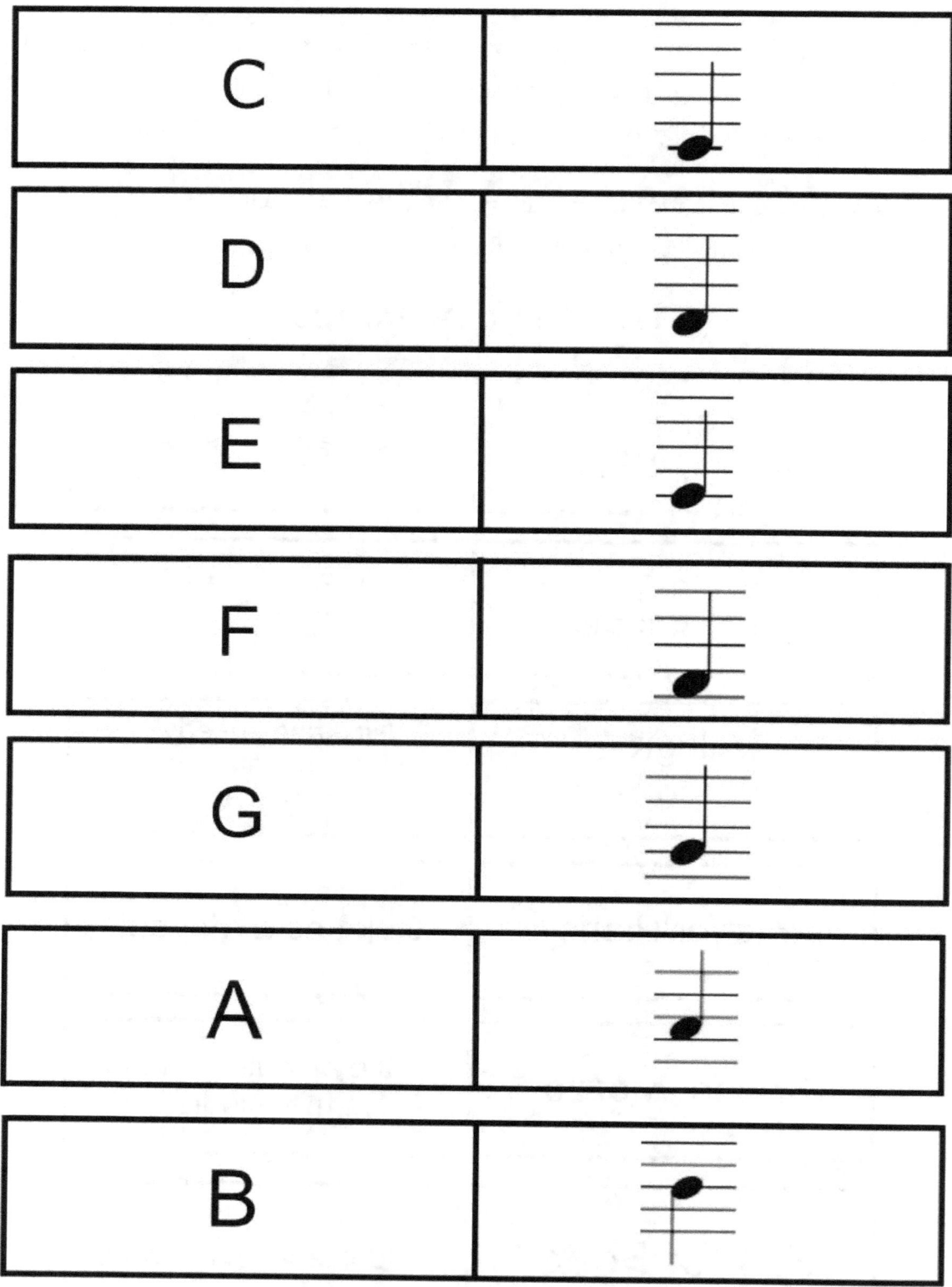

NOTES ON THE BASS STAFF

NOTES ON THE KEYBOARD

C	
D	
E	
F	
G	
A	
B	

NOTE VALUES AND REST VALUES

Quarter Note 1 Beat	♩
Half Note 2 Beats	♩
Dotted Half Note 3 Beats	♩.
Whole Note 4 Beats	𝅝
Quarter Rest 1 Beat of Silence	𝄽
Half Rest 2 Beats of Silence	▬
Whole Rest 4 Beats of Silence	▬
Eighth Note 1 Half Beat	♪

Hopefully, these fabulous flashcards will help to reinforce your musical knowledge! Cut them out and fold them along the centerline for fun guessing games with friends and family!

Oh wow! You've completed our final chapter together! Here is your final gold star! You've done a wonderful job at the beginning of your musical journey. Together we have conquered scales, sheet music, treble clefs, bass clefs, and just about everything in between! Hopefully, you can use this knowledge to blossom into a talented young musician! Good luck!

CONCLUSION

Beginner Piano Lessons for Kids

Taylor Kent W.

Congratulations! You have completed the first step on your musical journey through this book. We hope you had fun and learned a lot about playing the piano and reading sheet music. Remember, practice makes perfect! The key takeaway from this book is that with patience and perseverance, you can achieve anything you set your mind to. Just like how you mastered playing "Mary Had a Little Lamb," you can conquer any song you desire.

So, keep practicing your flashcards and scales, and let your hands glide over the piano keys! And once you're done, you have plenty of music to play with. Which song are you going to master first? "Ode to Joy"? "Silent Night"? "London Bridge"? The choice is yours.

We would love to hear about your progress, don't forget to leave a review to share your success with others! Thank you for joining us on this musical adventure, and we wish you the best of luck in your future musical endeavors!

Hey there, fellow music enthusiasts!

Are you ready to unlock the musical magic of the piano and embark on a musical journey like no other? If you've already enjoyed the delightful book "Beginner Piano Lessons for Kids," we need your help to spread the joy and encourage others to join in on the harmonious fun! By leaving a review, you'll help aspiring pianists find the perfect guide and contribute to a world filled with more beautiful music. Here's a question: have you ever considered how helping others can make a difference?

Leaving a review for "Beginner Piano Lessons for Kids" is your chance to deliver value to others. By sharing your experience, insights, and thoughts, you can help potential readers or listeners understand the true worth of this fantastic book. Whether you found it to be an absolute game-changer in your child's musical journey or simply a delightful resource filled with engaging lessons, your review will guide others in their decision-making process.

Your review is crucial because countless parents and young learners are searching for the perfect piano book but are overwhelmed by the vast selection available. Your words can shine a light on the brilliance of "Beginner Piano Lessons for Kids" and give them the confidence to take the plunge. Imagine the smiles on their faces as they discover the joy of creating music and the gratitude they'll feel toward you for sharing your thoughts!

So, here's our humble request: please take a moment to leave an honest review for "Beginner Piano Lessons for Kids" on your favorite online platform. Whether it's Amazon, Goodreads, or any other website where you purchased or discovered the book, your feedback matters immensely. It's super easy to do! Head to the book's page, scroll down to the review section and let your fingers dance across the keyboard as you type your thoughts.

By leaving a review, you become part of a beautiful community of music lovers passionate about sharing their experiences. Your words can profoundly impact someone else's life, sparking a love for music that will last a lifetime. Isn't it amazing to think that a few minutes of your time can positively impact someone else's journey?

So, what are you waiting for? Grab your favorite device, hop onto your preferred online platform, and tell the world how "Beginner Piano Lessons for Kids" has enriched your musical experience. Remember, your review can ignite a passion for piano in others and bring a symphony of joy to countless lives.

Thank you from the bottom of our musical hearts!

GLOSSARY

Beginner Piano Lessons for Kids

Taylor Kent W.

Cool Fact #5: Jimmy Liu, a boy from Tennessee, can play the piano with one hand and solve a Rubik's cube with the other!

How does Jimmy do it? Well, it's all about practice, my friend. Jimmy spends hours **Accelerando: Gradually** increasing the speed of the music.

Accent: Emphasizing a particular beat or note to make it stand out more.

Adagio: A slow and gentle tempo.

Allegro: A fast and lively tempo.

Arpeggio: A broken chord played one note at a time, usually in a specific pattern.

Bass clef: The symbol used to represent lower-pitched notes on the staff.

Beat: The steady pulse you can feel in a song or piece of music.

Chords: Two or more notes played together to create a harmony.

Clave: A rhythmic pattern that originates from Afro-Cuban music, consisting of two wooden sticks struck together to create a 3–2 or 2–3 pattern.

Clef: A symbol placed at the beginning of the staff to indicate the pitch range of the notes.

Crescendo: This means to gradually get louder. It's like when the volume of the music slowly increases.

Decrescendo: This means to gradually get softer. It's like when the volume of the music slowly decreases.

Diminuendo: This means to gradually get quieter. It's like when the volume of the music slowly fades away.

Dolce: Play the music sweetly and softly.

Dotted note: A note with a small dot next to it, which adds half of its original value to the note. For instance, if we look at a dotted quarter note, it will last for 1.5 beats instead of 1 beat.

Dynamics: The variations in volume or loudness of a piece of music. It refers to how the sound changes over time and can be indicated by different musical symbols, such as "piano" (soft) or "forte" (loud). Dynamics can add expression and emotion to a musical performance.

Forte: This means "loud." It's like when someone is talking or shouting really loudly.

Fortissimo: This means "very loud." It's like when someone is screaming or yelling at the top of their lungs.

Groove: The feel and energy of a rhythm, which can be funky, smooth, driving, or laid-back.

Ledger lines: Additional lines added above or below the staff to extend the range of notes that can be written.

Legato: Play the notes smoothly, connecting each one.

Lento: A slow and relaxed tempo.

Meter: The way beats are grouped together into larger units, such as 2 beats, 3 beats, or 4 beats.

Mezzo forte: This means "moderately loud." It's like when someone is speaking in a normal voice, not too loud or too soft.

Mezzo piano: This means "moderately soft." It's like when someone is speaking in a normal voice, not too loud or too soft.

Middle C: The note located in the center of the keyboard.

Octave: The distance between any two notes that share the same name.

Pedal: A foot-operated device that alters the sound of the piano by sustaining or softening the notes.

Phrase: A musical sentence or section that feels complete on its own, usually 4–8 measures long.

Piano: This means "soft." It's like when someone is whispering or speaking quietly.

Pianissimo: This means "very soft." It's like when someone is whispering so quietly that you can barely hear them.

Polyrhythm: Two or more rhythms played at the same time, creating a complex and layered sound.

Presto: A very fast tempo.

Rest: A pause in the music where no sound is played.

Rhythm: The way that beats are arranged in a song or piece of music to create a pattern.

Riff: A short, catchy melody or pattern repeated throughout a song or piece of music.

Ritardando: Gradually slowing down the speed of the music.

Scales: A series of notes played in a specific order to create a particular sound.

Sforzando: This means to play a note with a sudden, strong accent. It's like when someone slams a door shut loudly.

Shuffle: A rhythmic style where each beat is divided into three parts instead of two, creating a loping and swinging feel.

Staccato: Play the notes short and detached.

Staff: The five horizontal lines on which the musical notes are positioned.

Swing: A rhythmic style where the first beat of each pair is longer and the second beat is shorter, creating a bouncing, swinging feel.

Syncopation: A rhythmic pattern where the emphasis is on the off-beats or weaker beats, creating a jazzy or funky feel.

Tempo: The speed at which a song or piece of music is played.

Tie: A smooth curve that joins two or more notes with the same pitch, showing that they should be played together as a single, extended note.

Time signature: A symbol that tells you how many beats are in each measure and what type of note gets one beat.

Treble clef: The symbol used to represent higher-pitched notes on the staff.

Vivace: A very lively and fast tempo.

Volume: The loudness or softness of a sound. It can be controlled by adjusting how hard or softly an instrument is played or sung.

REFERENCES

Beginner Piano Lessons for Kids

Taylor Kent W.

All major and minor scales (including fingering for piano). (2020, August 19). OKTAV. https://stories.oktav.com/en/s/major-and-minor-scales

Allysia. (2016, October 8). *5 piano exercises for hand independence.* PianoTV.net. https://www.pianotv.net/2016/10/piano-exercises-hand-independence/

Andrea. (2012, April 12). *Piano student in need of a hand position fix?* Teach Piano Today. https://www.teachpianotoday.com/2012/04/12/how-to-correct-hand-position-in-young-piano-students-its-qa-day/

Andrea. (2013a, June 6). *5 fun piano finger warm-ups to build finger strength and dexterity.* Teach Piano Today. https://www.teachpianotoday.com/2013/06/06/how-to-teach-piano-to-kids-building-strength-and-dexterity-in-little-fingers/

Andrea. (2013b, November 26). *Does this photo make you cringe? Piano posture tips are here.* Teach Piano Today. https://www.teachpianotoday.com/2013/11/26/posture-perfect-tips-for-your-piano-kids/

Basic rhythm concepts you need to play piano. (n.d.). Piano Lesson on the Web. https://www.pianolessonsontheweb.com/blog/basic-rhythm-concepts-you-need-to-play-piano

Bass clef. (n.d.). Www.key-Notes.com. https://www.key-notes.com/blog/bass-clef#:~:text=To%20learn%20the%20lines%20of

Beginners level free piano sheet music. (n.d.). Www.8notes.com. https://www.8notes.com/piano/sheet_music/?difficulty=1

Beijing olympic games' piano auctioned at 22 mln yuan CCTV-International. (n.d.). English.cctv.com. http://english.cctv.com/20091123/102938.shtml

Care and maintenance of a piano:Tuning once a year - musical instrument guide. (n.d.). Www.yamaha.com. https://www.yamaha.com/en/musical_instrument_guide/piano/maintenance/maintenance002.html#:~:text=Pianos%20need%20regular%20tuning%20at

Catherine. (2015, July 13). *Why is piano a great instrument to learn first?* Gwinnettmusic. https://gwinnettmusic.com/piano-great-instrument-learn-first/

Cherie. (2021, August 25). *Learning piano fingers number is fun for kids!* Music Time Kid. https://musictimekid.com/piano-fingers-number/

Clap your hands: 16 clapping games for children's choir. (n.d.). Ashley Danyew. https://www.ashley-danyew.com/posts/2016/clap-your-hands-16-clapping-games-for-childrens-choir

EGBDF. (2023, May 3). Wikipedia. https://en.wikipedia.org/wiki/EGBDF

11 benefits of playing piano for kids (& when to start). (2022, August 1). Family KC. https://ifamilykc.com/blog/education-learning/benefits-playing-piano/

5 reasons your child should take piano lessons. (2016, September 9). One Little Project. https://onelittleproject.com/reasons-your-child-should-take-piano-lessons/

Free beginner piano sheet music. (n.d.). Makingmusicfun.net. https://makingmusicfun.net/htm/beginner_piano

Free childrens piano sheet music. (n.d.). Www.8notes.com. https://www.8notes.com/piano/childrens/sheet_music/

Fuzzy wuzzy, free, easy sheet music, 4 versions. (n.d.). Music for Music Teachers. https://www.music-for-music-teachers.com/fuzzy-wuzzy.html

Get piano lesson 5. (n.d.). Get Piano Lessons. https://get-piano-lessons.com/beginner-lessons-for-piano-left1/

Hand independence exercises for beginners. (2020, October 16). The Note. https://www.pianote.com/blog/beginner-hand-independence-exercises/?utm_campaign=15665178680&utm_source=google&utm_medium=cpc&utm_content=580325842206&utm_term=_&adgroupid=131111086283&gclid=CjwKCAiAioifBhAXEiwApzCztnT_mZ4eUIXdiNUJ7DmZxkb3WmJIy9ywwxkN26gYVGEdVxFyXXDSKhoC50cQAvD_BwE

Hot cross buns - free easy piano sheet music for right hand. (n.d.). Www.pianosongdownload.com. https://www.pianosongdownload.com/hotcrossbuns.html

How learning piano benefits your brain — 9 positives of piano. (n.d.). Pianu.com. https://pianu.com/blog/learning-piano-benefits-your-brain#:~:text=Learning%20Piano%20Actually%20Builds%20Brain%20Power&text=Breakthroughs%20in%20brain%20imaging%20have

How many black keys on a piano? how many white piano keys?(n.d.). Hoffman Academy. https://www.hoffmanacademy.com/blog/how-many-black-keys-on-a-piano/

How to count and play quarter notes on the piano. (n.d.). Instructables. https://www.instructables.com/How-to-Count-and-Play-Quarter-Notes-on-the-Piano/

How to read piano sheet music. (n.d.). Flowkey. https://www.flowkey.com/en/piano-guide/read-sheet-music

How to read sheet music: a step-by-step guide. (2014, April 11). Musicnotes. https://www.musicnotes.com/blog/how-to-read-sheet-music/

Is piano the best first instrument? (n.d.). Hoffman Academy. https://www.hoffmanacademy.com/blog/piano-a-great-place-to-begin/

Jackson, R. (2021, January 30). *What are piano keys made of? a complete guide.* Hello Music Theory. https://hellomusictheory.com/learn/what-are-piano-keys-made-of/

Jingle bells sheet music for beginner piano students. (n.d.). Music for Music Teachers. https://www.music-for-music-teachers.com/jingle-bells-sheet-music.html

Julia. (2009a). F*lashcards note values and rest values cut along solid line fold along dotted line.* https://www.theperfectstartforpiano.com/flashcards/PSflashcardsnotevaluesandrestvalues.pdf

Julia. (2009b). *Flashcards notes on the bass staff cut along solid line fold along dotted line.* https://www.theperfectstartforpiano.com/flashcards/PSflashcardsBassStaff.pdf

Julia. (2009c). *Flashcards notes on the keyboard cut along solid line fold along dotted line.* https://www.theperfectstartforpiano.com/flashcards/PSflashcardsnotesonthekeyboard.pdf

Julia. (2009d). *Flashcards notes on the treble staff cut along solid line fold along dotted line.* https://www.theperfectstartforpiano.com/flashcards/PSflashcardsTrebleStaff.pdf

Julia. (2009e). *Flashcards tempo and dynamics cut along solid line fold along dotted line.* https://www.theperfectstartforpiano.com/flashcards/PSflashcardstempoanddynamics.pdf

Kid's piano fingering 101. (n.d.). Piano by Number. https://pianobynumber.com/blogs/reading-room/kids-piano-fingering-101

L, M. (2021, November 12). *15 beautiful quotes every piano player will love.* TakeLessons Blog. https://takelessons.com/blog/quotes-about-piano#:~:text=

Learn how to read sheet music: notes for music. (2015, December 30). Take Note. https://blog.sheetmusicplus.com/2015/12/30/learn-how-to-read-sheet-music-notes/

Learning c position on the piano. (2014, July 16). Lessons in Your Home. https://lessonsinyourhome.net/blog/learning-c-position-piano/

Left hand piano exercise. (n.d.). Piano Lesson on the Web. https://www.pianolessonsontheweb.com/lefthand.html

Leslie. (n.d.). *The amazing race to middle c! a game for #teaching #piano.* Musical Bridges MT. https://www.musicalbridgesmt.com/2014/07/28/the-amazing-race-to-middle-c-a-game-for-teaching-piano/

Mary had a little lamb: right hand only. (n.d.). Www.pianosongdownload.com. https://www.pianosongdownload.com/maryhadalittlelambrighthand.html

megustaelpiano. (2016, July 8). *Piano technique for children: firm fingertips.* Me Gusta El Piano. https://megustaelpiano.com/piano-technique-for-children-firm-fingertips/

Middle c on the piano: why is it so important? (2021, January 25). Piano Blog by Skoove - Piano Practice Tips. https://www.skoove.com/blog/middle-c-on-piano/

Milne, E. (2011, August 10). *10 things you should do before your child begins piano lessons.* Elissa Milne. https://elissamilne.com/2011/08/10/10-things-you-should-do-before-your-child-begins-piano-lessons/

Mnemonic F A C E spells FACE in Music. (n.d.). Www.mnemonic-Device.com. https://www.mnemonic-device.com/music/face/

Mullett, S. (2014, May 29). *An easy way to teach kids rests.* Let's Play Music. https://www.letsplaykidsmusic.com/easy-way-to-teach-kids-rests/

Music for kids: piano playing basics. (n.d.). Www.ducksters.com. https://www.ducksters.com/musicforkids/piano_playing_basics.php#:~:text=The%20white%20keys%20represent%20the

The parents guide for kids starting to learn piano. (2020, July 2). Roland Resource Centre. https://rolandcorp.com.au/blog/parents-guide-for-kids-starting-piano

Patrick. (2017, June 9). *Piano fingering exercises: scales, chords, and more.* Musika Lessons Blog. https://www.musikalessons.com/blog/2017/06/piano-fingering-exercises/

Piano teaching games. (2012, May 29). Teach Piano Today. https://www.teachpianotoday.com/piano-teaching-games/

Praytor, A. (2022, May 21). *Left hand piano exercises to help your hands cooperate.* Hello Simply. https://www.hellosimply.com/blog/piano-beginner/left-hand-piano-exercises/

Ross, J. (n.d.). *Why does piano have black and white keys.* Joshua Ross Piano. https://joshuarosspiano.com/why-does-piano-have-black-and-white-keys/

Ross, J. (2020, January 17). *15 interesting piano facts you might not know!* Joshua Ross. https://joshuarosspiano.com/piano-facts/

Sheet music facts for kids. (n.d.). Kids.kiddle.co. https://kids.kiddle.co/Sheet_music

Steps and skips in piano music. (2020, December 8). Lessonsinyourhome.net. https://lessonsinyourhome.net/blog/steps-and-skips-in-piano-music-basic-music-intervals/#:~:text=When%20two%20notes%20have%20a

Tempo: Lesson for kids. (2020). Study.com. https://study.com/academy/lesson/tempo-lesson-for-kids.html

3-year-old piano prodigy set to perform at carnegie hall. (2021, June 2). NY Post. https://nypost.com/2021/06/02/3-year-old-piano-prodigy-set-to-perform-at-carnegie-hall/

36 easy piano songs for kids + free sheet music. (2022, February 21). Www.singing-Bell.com. https://www.singing-bell.com/easy-piano-songs-for-kids-free-sheet-music/

Top 3 left-hand piano exercises. (2020, November 20). The Note. https://www.pianote.com/blog/left-hand-piano-exercises/

Top 5 reasons why your child should learn piano at a young age | sparkling art piano studio in chicago. (n.d.). Sparkling Art Piano. https://www.sparklingartpiano.com/piano/top-5-reasons-learn-piano-young-age/#:~:text=Piano%20lessons%20and%20practice%20sessions

Top ten tips for good piano posture. (2014, April 22). Hoffman Academy. https://www.hoffmanacademy.com/blog/top-ten-tips-for-good-piano-posture/

Trevor. (2018, July 4). *A hands-on piano lesson activity to make rests meaningful.* Teach Piano Today. https://www.teachpianotoday.com/2018/07/04/how-your-piano-students-can-have-a-blast-stacking-cups-and-reinforcing-rests/

Twinkle twinkle little star free sheet music for piano. (n.d.). Music for Music Teachers. https://www.music-for-music-teachers.com/twinkle-twinkle.html

What kids understand about sheet music. (n.d.). Piano by Number. https://pianobynumber.com/blogs/readingroom/what-kids-understand-about-sheet-music

Whiz kid plays piano and solves rubik's cube simultaneously. (2020, July 21). NY Post. https://nypost.com/2020/07/21/whiz-kid-plays-piano-and-solves-rubiks-cube-simultaneously/

Yamaha. (n.d.). *The origins of the piano: The story of the piano's invention - musical instrument guide.* Www.yamaha.com. https://www.yamaha.com/en/musical_instrument_guide/piano/structure/#:~:text=The%20piano%20was%20invented%20by